From prehistoric cave art to abstract expressionism, from the Orient to the Western world —the six volumes in this series provide a panoramic view of man's achievements and his aspirations as they have been expressed in painting. The illustrations, all in full color, have been chosen with an eye to their freshness as well as their intrinsic worth: many of these masterpieces are virtually inaccessible to even the most dedicated art lover. Each volume is introduced by a leading authority in the field, who presents his insights in lucid, simple prose. Hans L. C. Jaffé, Professor of Modern Art at the University of Amsterdam, has edited the series with knowledge and care, to make *20,000 Years of World Painting* both a major esthetic experience and an exciting introduction to the history of art. The volumes in the series are:

MICHAEL LEVEY

Seventeenth and Eighteenth Century Painting

EDITED BY *Hans L. C. Jaffé*

20,000 Years of World Painting

VOLUME IV

Published by
DELL PUBLISHING CO., INC.
750 Third Avenue
New York, New York 10017

Laurel ® TM 674623, Dell Publishing Co., Inc.

Originally published as part of one volume
entitled 20,000 YEARS OF WORLD PAINTING

Reprinted by arrangement with
Harry N. Abrams, Incorporated

Manufactured in the Netherlands

First printing—1968

INTRODUCTION

The new fabric of the seventeenth and eighteenth centuries was woven from a rich Italian Renaissance past, dominated right up to 1800 by the giant Cinquecento figures of Raphael and Titian. Over this period there was gradual change rather than a break at any specific point. Titian seems to merge into Tintoretto, who already constructs a highly personal but Baroque world; the same is true of El Greco, whose stormy visionary art may be taken either as a final manifestation of the Renaissance or as a prelude to the full Baroque of the seventeenth century.

But there was a significant shift before the end of the sixteenth century, a shift destined to have important effects on nearly all the great European artists of the subsequent period. The finest flower of the Venetian Renaissance was withering: it expired with the death of Tintoretto in 1594. In the following year Annibale Carracci left his native Bologna for Rome where he was to settle. Already the other great North Italian painter, Caravaggio, was working in Rome. In 1600 Rubens arrived in Italy, and in the following year he visited Rome for the first time. Thus, by the beginning of the seventeenth century, Rome held a trinity of talent in three artists who stand as the founder-figures and representatives of their century.

As the century progressed Rome became more firmly entrenched as the artistic capital, not merely of Italy, but of all Europe. Venice retained the prestige of its great past; the sixteenth-century Venetian school exercised enormous and significant influence on virtually every great seventeenth-century painter. An oscillation was set up between the two poles, Venice and Rome. Sometimes they could be synthesized, but often they were directly opposed, and their dichotomy was expressed in such quarrels as those over color and drawing, or nature versus antiquity. The contribution of Venice remained, however, in the past, for during the seventeenth century it utterly failed to produce a great painter and only temporarily accommodated great painters from elsewhere. Rome was the modern meeting place of living talents, the most active center of patronage. Through it there passed Rubens and Van Dyck and Velázquez; Claude and Poussin settled there, as did Elsheimer. Of leading native painters, the Carracci and Cara- 5 vaggio were succeeded there by the generation of Domenichino, Reni, and Pietro da Cortona; and they in turn by Carlo Maratta, whose long career brings us well into the eighteenth century. For a hundred years Rome held the hegemony.

Although Rome was the dominant seventeenth-century city, it did not impose any specifically Roman style. Rather, it accommodated all styles and extremes, ranging from the almost rudely naturalistic to elevated classicism. It was as much the city of the Bamboccianti painters, with their predilection for genre, as it was the city of Sacchi and Poussin. Between these extremes Rome fostered a style of exciting, colorful, decorative art that was given the name of Baroque. In fact, the classical and the Baroque were not in clear-cut opposition to each other. They shared a common origin in the work of Annibale Carracci for the Farnese Gallery. Here, although the large frescoes are conceived as dignified easel pictures, the general effect of the elaborate medallions, *putti*, stucco figures, etc., is certainly Baroque in its illusionism. The curved ceiling is thought of as a long tunnel of painted canvas open at the corners to show the sky beyond. This feigning of space became typical of Baroque decoration and culminated in the aerial visions of Tiepolo in the eighteenth century. From Annibale Carracci there stemmed the two streams of imaginative history painting: the exuberant Baroque and the calmly classical—both very different from the powerful new naturalism of which Caravaggio was virtually the creator. It was here that a real division lay.

Caravaggio came to Rome with the earthy realistic tradition of North Italy behind him. His powerful, emotional, but highly realistic paintings immediately caused a sensation and had an influence which reverberated throughout Europe. While the Baroque conceives a world of almost delirious dreams, allegories, and mythologies (both sacred and profane), the art of Caravaggio is intensely concerned with ordinary humanity, with life on this earth; biblical stories are interpreted by him with vivid emphasis on the sheer facts—whether it be the humble birth of Christ or the bloody moment of St. John the Baptist's execution. This attachment to truth, the truth of things seen, gave painting a new function when it moved on to record the everyday facts about the world. Rembrandt and the whole Dutch School, Velázquez and Zurbarán, the Le Nain brothers, Rubens, all extend the actual subject matter of painting, very much as the philosophers and scientists of the period were extending knowledge about man and nature. The seventeenth century was conscious of challenging those medieval assumptions which had continued to guide Renaissance man—and this was as much of a rebellion as

6

Caravaggio's artistic one. The truths expressed by Galileo were deliberately contradicted by the Church, which broke the man but was eventually unable to resist his conclusions. Outside Italy religion was concerned more with justifying itself on moral than on miraculous grounds, and it is significant that Locke should write not only the *Essay Concerning Humane Understanding*, but also *The Reasonableness of Christianity*. With the coming of the eighteenth century, reason and reality in painting were to start struggling against the Baroque, and would ultimately triumph.

Caravaggio's work naturally appealed to many Northern painters also, bred in the Protestant tradition as well as in the tradition of pungently realistic painting. Though he did not positively teach, he was in effect the master of a whole school of Italian artists, at Naples as well as Rome, and of the Spaniard Ribera as well. French and Dutch painters returned to their native lands to practice a Caravaggesque realism. Landscape had already become a subject for art in the work of Altdorfer and Pieter Bruegel the Elder. In Caravaggio's Rome, the German Elsheimer played an important part in creating intimate, poetic, but realistic small pictures of landscapes where the whole atmosphere is sensitively observed. He influenced Rubens, who was also his close friend, and later Claude. In his miniature-like way, he revolutionized landscape painting in Italy, emphasizing the facts of the natural world as Caravaggio emphasized those of ordinary humanity.

While Caravaggio asserted the new, Annibale Carracci was partly asserting the traditional. The influence of Raphael was strong in him, and stronger still in his pupils. Unlike Caravaggio, he was a gifted teacher. The classical elements in his style are emphasized and reiterated by Domenichino (who came from Bologna to work near him in Rome) and Domenichino in turn was to exercise a decisive effect on Poussin's art. This was a tranquil, somewhat withdrawn world in which the painter was often more at ease in private commissions for small pictures than in large-scale decorations. A more confident and public classicism was expressed by Guido Reni, trained in the Carracci Academy at Bologna, whose late work is a positive triumph of the calm and cool-colored.

But also studying as a young man under Annibale Carracci was Lanfranco who, along with Pietro da Cortona, created the high Roman Baroque style of the seventeenth century. It is epitomized, on a vast scale, by Cortona's ceiling for the Palazzo Barberini in which he glorifies the Barberini family in allusion and allegory, and involves the whole cosmos with its fortunes. This style was to travel outside Italy too—had already traveled earlier in Rubens' work—but required princely patrons and large-scale 7 areas to make its full effect. Even more audacious illusionistic effects were to be devised by artists like Padre Pozzo. The eighteenth century was to see these tendencies developed, not so much in Italy as in Germany and Austria—the last flights from the real into the dizzily irrational.

In seventeenth-century Italy the oscillating tendencies between naturalism and the "High" style, between Titian and Raphael, are most clearly seen in the work of Guercino. He was, significantly, not to establish himself successfully at Rome and had to retire from the center to the periphery. His early work is strongly Venetian in color and handling, and often charmingly realistic. It probably seemed somewhat undignified to Roman eyes, and Guercino returned in 1623 to his native Cento, near Bologna. In the subsequent years he evolved from his Venetian manner a calmer and more classical style, based very strongly on Reni. After Reni's death in 1642, Guercino moved to Bologna and painted in a completely classical, idealized manner, from which all the fire and poetry had fled. In him Raphael had conquered Titian; but it had not been a victory for art.

One genius was able to assimilate without difficulty the lessons of these two great men: Rubens. In the same way, he was able to draw from the two artistic streams of Caravaggio and Annibale Carracci to such an extent that it might be said paradoxically that he was the greatest Italian painter of the century. He is undoubtedly the most typical figure of the period, with a tremendous Baroque invention combined with a tremendous grasp on reality. It is symbolically right that he should have been an active traveler in Spain, France, England, and one whose art was in demand wherever he went. Rubens drew together all the strands from the past and from the early years of the seventeenth century. He became in turn a founder-figure exercising tremendous influence on the great artists who eventually came after, and exercising it far beyond his own century. He is the master of Watteau in the eighteenth century, and of Delacroix in the nineteenth.

His immediate influence in his native Flanders stimulated a whole school of followers and imitators, mostly caricaturing his vigor and realism. Only Van Dyck escaped in another direction, again under direct impressions of Italian art, into a fluent and refined painting which is less vigorous than Rubens' and more wistfully romantic. Van Dyck tends to adorn rather than explore truth, and he remains perhaps the least typical seventeenth-century painter—certainly the least typical Northern painter. Strong attachment to the facts of life in Flanders is the root of Teniers'
8 art; his peasant scenes are unprettified (but often sensitively

painted). They are more sober than Bruegel's and are part of the whole European movement toward recording reality which reaches its culmination in Holland.

Here the Baroque made little appeal. Instead it was Caravaggism, brought back from Italy by artists like Terbrugghen; and the Catholic city of Utrecht was a center for this style. Honthorst, too, had been influenced by Caravaggio in Rome, and he settled at Utrecht, becoming one of the few internationally known Dutch painters of this day. In Holland it is Caravaggism, tamed and made to have less of an assault on the emotions, which leads on to the work of Vermeer. It is contained in Rembrandt, the pupil of Lastman who worked in Rome in the first decade of the seventeenth century and who was formed by the pictures of Elsheimer and Caravaggio.

Rembrandt himself is the solitary exception among the great seventeenth-century painters in that he never visited Italy. But the Italian influence was inescapable and, indeed, was welcomed by him. He owed no allegiance specifically to Rome. Like Rubens, he too assimilated rather more from Titian than from Raphael. But elements from both were in his art: for his *Self-Portrait* of 1640 in the National Gallery in London, he borrowed from Raphael's *Castiglione* as well as from Titian. There is even a period of Baroque drama in Rembrandt. His refusal to travel is expressive of the deep attachment of his art to the life and conditions of his native country. All the categories of Dutch art—landscape, portrait, still life, genre—are contained in Rembrandt's work. His drawings reveal the sheer range of his art almost better than do his paintings. He is forever re-creating his environment, his family, and himself. A whole existence can be reconstructed from Rembrandt's art: a private, often unhappy life, but, thanks to art, always vivid. Rembrandt's reality is increasingly a psychological one. His early paintings show him fascinated by the appearance of things and people; light dramatically illumines surfaces. But gradually he goes beneath the surface appearance; the lighting is less abrupt and more subtle in its exploration. His portraits become less showy and more responsive to the sitter as a thinking, suffering human being. Life is no longer a record of outward fact, but an experience savored within.

For lesser Dutch painters technical competence combined with observation to produce an art that clearly mirrored outward facts—the placid landscape, the ever present sea, the market place, the breakfast table. These, too, present an unparalleled report, in pictures, of the painter's environment. Dutch patrons asked in effect to be reassured that what they saw was seen by their artists, too. They were less concerned with feeling, and only certain painters—like Ruisdael—were able to record natural phenomena with any vein of poetry. In Vermeer it is almost a superreality which has replaced the ordinary: an environment in which shapes are painted with appreciation of their abstract beauty—preluding the beautiful abstracted reality of Braque.

Vermeer seems to belong with that grave philosophical exploration of reality that is the seventeenth century's preoccupation, and more profoundly personal to it than the outward display of the Baroque. It is the same nearly mathematical effect that in Spain was achieved by Zurbarán, but which is equally present in Velázquez. He too looks to the world about him for his subject matter. His few mythological pictures simply put ancient Greece onto solid seventeenth-century Spanish earth. Although Velázquez painted with Titianesque freedom, the results are more pondered and grave. Reality is observed with a detachment that is scientific. The painter steps back from the sitter and scrutinizes him or her to produce an effect of absolute verisimilitude, itself achieved only by an effort of will. Although the final result in a painting by Velázquez gives a powerful sense of logic and rightness and truth, these have been reached only through experiment. Thus it is probably quite wrong to identify the dispassionate appearance of Velázquez' pictures with dispassion in the painter himself. It might even be that he had a natural impulse to record the immediate impression on his senses—for which he was superbly gifted—but controlled this impulse in the search for a "truth" that was more than immediate. The authority of his pictures comes from this rigor; each object is placed with an exact sense of interval and space. Fluency in the actual paint conceals thought and gives everything a deceptively improvised air. In Zurbarán there is a heavy application of paint which increases the air of timelessness and gravity; reality is formalized much more patently than in Velázquez. Even Murillo, though much sweeter and more decorative, is attached to the realistic tendency of the century; his once popular genre pictures have a strong basis of fact in everyday street scenes. If he prettifies poverty and low life, he is at least aware of it.

Flanders, Holland, and Spain were all separated from Italy by geography or politics, but France was closely bound to Italy by uneasy proximity and by religion. These were the two countries which most fruitfully practiced artistic exchange. Italian painters were active in Paris, while both Claude and Poussin preferred Rome to their own country. French painting presents the same divisions as Italian painting at the period. An early generation of French painters, including Valentin and Vouet, worked in Rome and took back Caravaggism to France. There evolved a specifically French realism, represented by Georges de La Tour (who probably owed something to the Utrecht painters) and by the Le Nain brothers. In them religious subjects are treated as humble genre, while genre itself takes on the dignity of showing the poor as they are: neither funny nor to be sentimentalized. There are no anecdotes, but simply depictions of peasant life.

The Le Nain brothers and La Tour remained obscure painters. They represent the opposite of the state Baroque style which reached its most sumptuous flowering under Louis XIV. Vouet's decorative abilities found full scope in rich private houses and the royal palaces, and this French Baroque continued under his pupil Lebrun, whose chief work is the decoration of the Hall of Mirrors (Galerie des Glaces) at Versailles. This style was not interrupted in 1700, and it is the forerunner of the Rococo in France.

By remaining in Rome, Poussin and Claude detached themselves from state patronage; they had the freedom of being *déraciné* and they created their own highly personal solutions. Poussin moved away from the first Romantic influence of Venetian painting to a much more cerebral, classical type of picture—the most classical ever created. It is strongly based on reality, and Poussin showed a preference for history over mythology. It was with almost archaeological intent that he re-created the antique world, and with profoundly philosophic implications. While he schematized and formalized the real—people and buildings and landscape—it always remained alive and never became insipid. In a more obvious way Claude poeticized reality. Sustained for subject matter entirely by the Roman Campagna, Claude drew his inspiration from nature, though what he finally created was vision blended with fact. Both painters ignored the brilliantly colored, exciting Baroque world that was being created in the Rome they lived in, and without overtly rebelling against society, asserted the artist's right to paint what he wishes.

It is an irony that by the end of the seventeenth century the movement of *Poussinisme* should have stood for a restrictive attitude to painting and thus have been brought into antagonism with the movement of *Rubénisme*. Yet, beneath these names, it was really the old dichotomy. Nature was now more important than antiquity, and draftsmanship more important than color. Throughout early eighteenth-century Europe, *Rubénisme* triumphed, standing for that tail end of the Baroque whirlwind that is the Rococo. The shift in Italy was back to Venice, where a new renaissance was taking place: Canaletto, Guardi, Rosalba Carriera, the Ricci, Pellegrini, Piazzetta, and, most triumphant of all, Tiepolo, showed that Venice again had painters who could serve the world. Simultaneously, Paris felt an impetus to new freedom, and the death of Louis XIV in 1715 accelerated the process. Venice and Paris were in close artistic contact these early years. France produced one genius to enshrine the new freedom, Watteau: himself drawing on the twin sources of Rubens and the Italian tradition, but creating one positive new category of picture, the *fête galante*, in which mood is more important than subject. Watteau intimates, without actually proclaiming, the death of the history picture. His work has no elevated moral lesson; it is not usually on a large scale, and his patrons were private people, often his friends. What separates it from the charming but trivial contemporary decorators in France and Italy is its serious psychological and emotional power; for all its miniature scale it is always concerned with people, not puppets. It may be set, as it were, in a theater—but it is the theater of the human heart.

Meanwhile, Rococo decorators flourished. The Italians, especially the Venetians, were everywhere in demand: more were employed outside Italy than in it. Germany and Austria were particularly receptive to the Rococo and produced their own superb Rococo architecture, as well as talented painters like Maulpertsch to decorate its interiors. Germany offered to Tiepolo the greatest opportunity—and he made magnificent use of it—when he frescoed the Prince-Bishop's Palace at Würzburg in 1750–53. Though he painted Apollo, the sun-god, in full glory at the center of his ceilings, in fact twilight was quickly to follow. Tiepolo represents the apogee of the Baroque—and its end. His radiant people, so at home as they float in the clouds of enchanted skies, are the last inhabitants of that sphere. Mythologizing was about to end. Morality was to demand "truth" in art, and the Rococo was to be condemned as false.

In France the career of Boucher runs nearly parallel to Tiepolo's. Both were to be condemned by advanced taste before their deaths in 1770. Boucher's gallant, charming, and decorative pictures do not quite create a convincing climate of their own, but they celebrate a dream of voluptuousness and artifice. His people are not supposed to be real; they are so many beautiful bodies, ripe as fruit and with the same bloom, arranged to give the spectator pleasure. Boucher has no other standard but to please. His landscapes are equally disposed so as to delight—created to look not like the real countryside, but like a playful countryside made out of silk and feathers. Truth gives place to decorative emphasis. The landscapes are as much a deception as the visionary skies painted by Rococo artists on real ceilings: feigning the existence of what everyone knows does not exist.

Such a mood was increasingly out of accord with eighteenth-century enlightenment. The previous century had produced a vast body of pictures which conveyed facts about our ordinary and visible environment. Now the eighteenth century wanted pictures which would combine with progressive opinion and the other arts to teach man how he should live in the world he had made.

It was in England—so much admired politically by the European intelligentsia—that the first painter of modern moral subjects was to be produced: William Hogarth. Hogarth was influenced by the lively touch of the French Rococo painters, and tried to emulate the Italian Baroque history painters. But his best and most influential pictures were those scenes of topical life which narrated a complete moral story—positive novels in paint. Thus painting took on an engaged tone and purpose. It was dealing with the reality of life, satirizing the bad and praising the good; above all, it had recovered some purpose. In recovering this it did not always matter how artistically good the actual pictures were. This confusion of morals and art is one reason why the elaborate but badly painted story-telling compositions of Greuze were greeted with such praise by Diderot and his contemporaries. Greuze had no ability to satirize; his penchant was rather for sentimental depictions of village life which were meant to touch the heart. In fact, they were as false as the very pictures by Boucher which Diderot castigated; but their professed intention made them seem morally better.

Although it is hard to pardon Greuze for his ambiguous attitude toward his milkmaids and village girls with their artfully disarranged clothing, it is easy to appreciate the urgent feeling of intelligent people that art must come down to the ground and concern itself with the human condition. The eighteenth century inspired the painter to express this humanity without posturing, and without any program of revolt. Chardin, exemplifying this attitude, has in his genre scenes all the integrity of Poussin's art, and the same rigorous control, subordinating reality to a beautifully plotted scheme. Chardin painted with a heavy yet smooth brush stroke, which gives every object its weight, its place, and which somehow seems to capture its essence. He asserts permanence after the fluidity of the Rococo. Time stops; nothing moves; forever a woman holds a shopping bag, a boy blows a bubble, a child reads. No lesson is preached, but life is seen as at once intensely intimate and humble. In his still lifes Chardin transcends again the trivia of assorted objects, making a formal pattern and a satisfying subject out of two apples, a copper pan, and a white earthenware jug.

As the Rococo was really only the tail end of the Baroque, so its growing rival, the Neoclassic, was really the tail end of seventeenth-century classicism—with a sting in the shape of David. Rome had remained largely unaffected by the Rococo. It was ready to harbor the Neoclassic movement, first apparent in Batoni, gathering strength with Mengs, and then in full force under David. It was in Rome in 1785 that David created and exhibited *The Oath of the Horatii*, seen and immediately applauded by artists of all nations. Here at last was dignified reality, combined with a moral lesson from the great days of a great republic. It asserted truths, both visual and moral, in its attempted accuracy of detail and noble patriotic sentiment. It is a consciously revolutionary picture, and a few years later the revolution was to come, with David one of its most eager participants. Europe underwent an emotional upheaval which left artists clinging not to programs, but to their own consciousnesses. Society existed as something to withdraw from completely, and the Romantic, utterly private vision takes the place of moral lessons.

The eighteenth century's interest in humanity made it naturally responsive to portraiture. Portraits were no longer restricted to being of upper-class and royal sitters; everyone was painted, and painted *en déshabillé*, or working, or relaxing among friends. State portraits and allegorical ones, like those of Nattier, increasingly seemed too pompous and unreal. Most of the Neoclassicists—such as Batoni, Mengs, and, supremely, David—were good portrait painters. In England the relaxed and graceful genius of Gainsborough represents the quintessence of the civilized, unassertive portrait. His men and women, though at times more elegant than in reality, never try to impose their characters; they descend from Van Dyck in their easy negligence. Reynolds is more concerned to state something about his sitters, to make each portrait a comment on character. They play in art their roles in life and, paradoxically, this leads on to the Romantic portraiture of Lawrence and the early nineteenth century where each sitter acts out his personal drama; and Napoleon poses as the world conqueror.

The last great eighteenth-century painter, the first of the nineteenth century, is Goya. He, too, is obsessed by humanity, mocking of its vices, but angry as well. The penetration seen in his portraits (themselves influenced partly by mezzotints of English eighteenth-century work) and his refusal to be imposed on by outward rank reach biting revolutionary depths. He moves from the decorative genre of his early work into closer contact with people, recording man's brutality to man, and the cruelty

of the French invaders of Spain who yet were welcome after the

Bourbon monarchy. Thus he—alone of eighteenth-century painters—reached down into the psychological dilemma of mankind. All those professions of wanting to be good and noble did not impose on Goya; he knew that reason is always struggling with the blackness of the human heart. His etchings and drawings reveal what humanity is really like; and he holds up a mirror not to the superficiality of daily life, but to the real reality of existence: its urge to destroy. His last pictures portray the nightmare of a world gone mad, a world we can recognize only too clearly as modern and our own.

EL GRECO (1541–1614) *St. John the Evangelist* · Detail from *The Crucifixion* · 1594–1604 · Oil on canvas · $35\frac{1}{4} \times 30\frac{3}{8}''$ · The Prado, Madrid

El Greco represents the fusion of several High Renaissance styles into a personal style that strongly preludes the Baroque. A stormy spirituality agitates the emotional figure of St. John who seems to have no more substance than a candle flame, wrapped in a strange drapery and with a single flamelike hand raised in horror. The certainties of High Renaissance classicism have been exchanged for a deliberately disturbed art. El Greco, born in Crete, had trained in Venice and must have been influenced by Tintoretto. In 1577 he is recorded at Toledo where he lived until his death. His increasingly mystic and private pictures reveal the mind of an artist working in isolation.

EL GRECO *Cardinal Juan de Tavera* · 1609–14 · Oil on canvas · 40⅛ × 32⅝″ · Hospital of St. John the Baptist, Toledo

While this portrait is certainly a vivid portrayal, and may be a good likeness of the sitter, the picture is instinct with the painter's personality. It is probable that El Greco used Tavera's death mask for the portrait, as Tavera had died in 1545. A moon-blanched light illumines the long bony head and turns pale the stiff folds of the cardinal's cape. He rests his hand on a heavy book which lies horizontally on a table that slopes steeply toward the spectator. The effect is to increase the sense of height: the sitter narrows to this tall thin figure, topped by that white luminous face with its haunted eyes, dark in the cadaverous eye sockets.

17

EL GRECO *The Virgin* · Detail from *The Holy Family* · Oil on
canvas · 44⅛ × 41⅜″ · Hospital of St. John the Baptist, Toledo

An earlier painting than *Cardinal Tavera*, *The Virgin* shows El
Greco still very conscious of his Venetian training. The color is
less mysterious than it later becomes, and there is something of
Bassano, as well as Tintoretto, in the almost roughly sketched-in
features, the brush strokes of the hair and the crackling folds of
drapery round the Virgin's head. The lighting is less erratic and
18 emotional than in many other pictures by El Greco.

EL GRECO *The Crucifixion* · 1590–95 · Oil on canvas · 70 × 42½″ · Zuloaga Museum, Zumaya

Before El Greco, Tintoretto had conceived the Crucifixion as virtually a Baroque drama in which the whole world seems gathered at Calvary. This concept is borrowed but transformed by El Greco. The figure of Christ on the Cross fills the whole composition, giving an effect of his being thrust into the sky, raised far above the bleak earth. It is a moment of utter isolation for Christ. But the cosmos expresses something of this tremendous moment of its Creator's Crucifixion. The black sky is riven by jagged cracks of light; the earth seems shaken by the event. 19

EL GRECO *St. John's Vision of the Apocalypse* · c. 1613 · Oil on canvas · 88⅛ × 76⅜″ · Metropolitan Museum of Art, New York

El Greco naturally responded to the visionary. The allusive, highly pictorial imagery of the Apocalypse inspired him to effortless fantasy, reworking St. John's narrative in his own highly charged terms. St. John himself is seen at the left almost crucified by emotion, while in a lunar landscape those "who have come out of great tribulation" receive white robes. The robes are like ectoplasm, windy vaporous shapes similar to the vague clouds that fill the sky. A wind seems to shake all the gesticulating forms. Old ideas of formal composition have been replaced by this dynamic painting where emotion has dictated the lopsided design. St. John is almost as visionary as what he sees: the whole scene has been heightened, literally, by the tall figures, and then given an eerie quality by sulfurous green lighting which wavers over flesh and draperies.

ANNIBALE CARRACCI (1560–1609) *Venus and Adonis* · Oil on canvas · 85⅜ × 96⅞″ · Kunsthistorisches Museum, Vienna

Annibale Carracci, the greatest of the Carracci, the Bolognese family of painters, is the earliest of the creators of the Baroque. His style was woven out of elements from the great Cinquecento artists who had preceded him, among them Raphael, the Venetians, and Correggio. *Venus and Adonis* shows what he evolved out of this heritage, making an art highly colored and dignified, despite playful touches. The whole subject here is an homage to Venetian painting, but the cupid at the left is clearly inspired by Correggio. The actual draftsmanship is, however, very much more careful than in a Venetian picture, the poses are carefully studied, and the result is an almost sculptural plasticity in the bodies of Venus and, especially, Adonis.

Annibale Carracci *Silenus and Pan* · Tempera on wood
14 × 32″ · National Gallery, London

This picture shows, on a small scale, the decorative gifts of
Annibale at their height. It comes from a harpsichord—being
part of the keyboard lid—and the subject of music is thus ap-
propriate. Almost certainly it was painted in Rome, but the
original fortunate owner of the harpsichord is not known. On
the walls of the Farnese Gallery Annibale had shown how effort-
lessly he could devise a large-scale scheme of decoration and
enter the classical, mythological world. With equal ease he depicts
here the silvery rustic setting where the young god plays his
pipes to the ogling, lecherous Silenus. It is an Arcadian atmosphere that he captures, artificial but highly decorative, and painted in dry tempera to give the effect of fresco.

ANNIBALE CARRACCI *Domine, Quo Vadis?* · Oil on panel · 30 × 21″ · National Gallery, London

Rome gave new dignity to Annibale Carracci's art. It remained no less painterly but its impetuous qualities were restrained. Detail was broadened and simplified under the direct contact with Raphael's work. The broad polished draperies of the *Domine, Quo Vadis?*, the unparticularized cross, and—above all—the careful posing of the two figures reveal the new classical strain. Everything is tightly organized. It is hard to say how Annibale himself would have developed this aspect of his art, for his increasing ill-health and premature death prevented him from playing the personal part to which his talent entitled him.

ANNIBALE CARRACCI *Flight into Egypt* · c. 1603 · Oil on canvas
$47\frac{1}{2} \times 88\frac{1}{2}$″ · Doria Pamphili Gallery, Rome

This lunette is among Annibale's late works in Rome, one of the
series of sacred subjects planned by him for the chapel of the
Palazzo Aldobrandini, but of which he himself executed only this
single one; the remainder were the work of his pupils Domenichino and Albani. While there is strong poetry in the group of
the Holy Family—the donkey having been given a temporary
respite from carrying anyone—the landscape has become more
important and insistent than in the *Domine, Quo Vadis?* for
example. It is a completely organized spatial scene in which the
eye is led down to the water, across it, and over the undulating
slopes to the satisfying square buildings on the far hill. This is a
new type of art, preluding not only Domenichino, but the great
achievements of Poussin and Claude when they too settled in
24 Rome some years later.

CARAVAGGIO (1573–1610) *A Basket of Fruit* · c. 1590 · Oil on canvas · 18 × 25½″ · Pinacoteca Ambrosiana, Milan

The abrupt naturalism that enters seventeenth-century art with Michelangelo Merisi da Caravaggio is proclaimed by this painting. Although the ground has been repainted, there can be no doubt that this is not a fragment but a picture in its own right. The subject of still life—which was to become so popular in the seventeenth century—was already created by Caravaggio in Rome about 1596. He had been born in the small Lombard town of Caravaggio, whence his name, and trained in Milan. Like nearly every other great artist of the period, he was attracted to Rome where his first important patron was Cardinal del Monte, for whom this still life was painted. Caravaggio paints all the textures of leaves, fruit, basket with *trompe l'oeil* realism, deliberately thrusting the objects forward in the picture plane so that the effect is of an actual basket, heavy with fruit, placed on a real ledge just in front of the spectator.

25

CARAVAGGIO *The Fortuneteller* · Oil on canvas · 39 × 51⅝″ · The Louvre, Paris

The Giorgionesque tradition of sitters in fancy dress is here taken up by Caravaggio and reworked in his own idiom. The actual painting is a deliberate piece of virtuosity, with brilliant handling of white—a color which always appealed to Caravaggio—and with positive enjoyment in the showy effect of rich velvet, feathers, and linen. The boy is of a type particularly appealing to the painter: he and very similar models also appear in other pictures. Here he is dressed up as a gallant, and the act of having his fortune read is given a consciously erotic overtone as the girl exchanges glances with him. Absolute simplicity of background helps to concentrate attention on this encounter, and an ordinary moment of daily life is heightened by psychological tension.

26

CARAVAGGIO *Boy with a Basket of Fruit* · c. 1610 · Oil on canvas · 26 × 20⅝″ · Borghese Gallery, Rome

Caravaggio's interest in daily life is not indiscriminate. It was only certain aspects which attracted him. Even when his models are beggar boys, they have been refined into something deliberately glamorous, as rich in their way as the fruit they often carry. These early pictures—like the present one—are not ambitious as compositions. The figure is usually alone, shown only half-length and seldom in action. But part of Caravaggio's revolutionary realism comes from choosing such ordinary sitters and from making the subject of this picture no more than that of a boy with a basket of fruit. No longer does the painter restrict himself to religious pictures or portraits of respectable citizens. Although Caravaggio himself was violent and quarrelsome, he found important patrons and his pictures were sought after.

CARAVAGGIO *David with Goliath's Head* · c. 1606 · Oil on canvas ·
26 × 25⅝″ · Borghese Gallery, Rome

Caravaggio's later pictures, of which this is one, show the marked
evolution of his art. There is no longer a hard clear light bathing
every object, but a thick dusky twilight from which figures
emerge with poignancy. Feeling is emphasized in a new and
emotional way. Here David seems to suffer from his deed of
killing Goliath. He is not triumphant but mournful as he gazes
at the giant's head—a head which is traditionally thought
to be a portrait of Caravaggio himself. The actual painting too
has become muted and less aggressive; enamel-bright colors
have given way to these subtle tones where the whites are
grayish. The paint is laid on thinly, to suit his quiet mood. The
effect is a fresh revolution in religious painting, anticipating the
achievements of Rembrandt.

ADAM ELSHEIMER (1578–1610) *Tobias and the Angel* · Oil on copper · 7½ × 10¾" · National Gallery, London

Adam Elsheimer brought his own revolution to Rome in the early years of the seventeenth century. Born in Germany, he traveled to Venice and then settled in Rome where he was to die prematurely. In his short working life he created a new type of landscape art in small pictures where the figures are subordinated to the setting and where the setting is romantic, natural landscape observed with subtle feeling for atmosphere. He responded particularly to twilit and night scenes and to the poetry of dark woodlands and overshadowed water. In this picture Tobias and the angel return home through such a quiet countryside, delineated down to the minute details of plants and leaves. This is probably one of Elsheimer's last pictures, where the figures gain new importance in the composition. Elsheimer was a friend of Rubens and an influence on Claude.

DOMENICHINO (1581–1641) *Girl with a Unicorn* · c. 1602 · Fresco ·
Farnese Palace, Rome

Domenichino was one of the leading pupils of Annibale Carracci
in Rome, working with him on the frescoes for the Farnese
Palace in the opening years of the seventeenth century. *Girl with
a Unicorn* is one of Domenichino's frescoes done at this early
date, and one of his most spontaneously attractive works. There
is already apparent in it something of Domenichino's tender,
melancholy style. His art is happiest when not concerned with
action but with idealizing figures and landscape into calmly
classical compositions—and it was to have a considerable impact
on Poussin. Domenichino's own nature was withdrawn and
somewhat difficult. His art was out of sympathy with the Baroque
exuberance that was coming into fashion in the later part of
his life. He retired from Rome to work at Naples, but his last
commission there was hindered by the jealousy of Neapolitan
30 painters.

DOMENICO FETTI (c. 1589–1623) *The Good Samaritan* · Oil on
panel · 23⅝ × 17″ · Metropolitan Museum of Art, New York

Born in Rome, Domenico Fetti was influenced first by Caravaggio and Elsheimer. By 1613 he had settled in Mantua where
the Gonzaga collection of Venetian pictures, particularly, must
have influenced him, and also Rubens' pictures. Hist most original paintings are small-scale works, usually illustrations of the
Parables (as here). He repeated these compositions in several
versions, and *The Good Samaritan* is one of the most frequently
repeated. The subject is treated in a simple, direct way as pure
genre, with emphasis on the landscape setting.

GUERCINO (1591–1666) *The Incredulity of St. Thomas* · Oil on
canvas · 45½ × 55½″ · National Gallery, London

Francesco Barbieri, called Guercino, was born at Cento, near
Bologna, and he spent a considerable portion of his working life
there. His art also lies outside the main currents of the seventeenth century, being blended partly from Caravaggio and from
the sixteenth-century Venetians. His later pictures are inspired
by the example of Guido Reni and aim at a calmer and more
classical manner. His early pictures—like *The Incredulity of St.
Thomas*—have opulent coloring and a richly handled paint surface. There is a direct emotional "attack" in the dramatic, moving
depiction of the shadowy Apostle thrusting his fingers into the
wound on Christ's brightly lit body. The composition is itself a
drama of contrast between light and darkness, echoed by the
tender yielding expression of Christ and the jutting, almost aggressive profile of St. Thomas. The picture has all the vigor of
32 the full Baroque.

BERNARDO CAVALLINO (1622–54) *St. Cecilia* · 1645 · Oil on canvas · 24⅜ × 19⅝″ · National Museum, Naples

Bernardo Cavallino lived and worked at Naples but his art is not typically Neapolitan. Its refined and personal nature seems a reflection of the painter's own, and its delicate tonality is very unlike the harsh chiaroscuro of most Neapolitan artists. Cavallino's figures have an elegant, elongated grace and are posed with almost exaggerated refinement. St. Cecilia becomes expressionistic in her attitude as the angel appears to her. Little is known about Cavallino's life and the evolution of his art. *St. Cecilia* is his only signed and dated picture, and well represents the silvery grace of an art that was still evolving when plague killed the artist.

BERNARDO STROZZI (1581–1644) *Man Blowing a Fife* · c. 1623–25 ·
Oil on canvas · 34¼ × 26¾″ · Palazzo Rosso, Genoa

Strozzi might almost be a Northern painter, judging from his
pictures, and the influence of Rubens on him was decisive.
Strozzi was born and trained in Genoa, but later settled in Venice.
His vigorous Northern style is patent in the picture here, with its
emphasis on a sort of rustic realism. The almost uncouth pose of
the wrinkled, puffing old man has a vigor that is nearly ludicrous.
He blows his wooden, countrified instrument at the spectator in
arresting fashion, and the picture is noisy with the sound. Like
Caravaggio, and like so many of his contemporaries, Strozzi is
anxious to record the ordinary, humble reality that he knows—
34 and record it in the most effective way.

ORAZIO GENTILESCHI (1563–1639) *The Luteplayer* · c. 1626 · Oil on canvas · 56⅝ × 51⅛″ · National Gallery of Art, Washington, D.C.

Orazio Gentileschi is one of the few painters influenced by Caravaggio who actually knew Caravaggio personally. But his art had little of the great painter's force. From Caravaggio he acquired an interest in textures and an ability to use white—as in the present picture—with decorative effect. Gentileschi was in fact hardly more than a pleasing decorator with a certain response to color. Even the luteplayer is strangely disengaged, playing her lute at an awkward angle—not so much playing as posing with it. Gentileschi's brightly colored, not too serious style was successful far beyond Italy: he worked at the royal courts of France and England and was important as a disseminator of the Caravaggesque style throughout Europe.

Pietro da Cortona (1596–1669) Sketch for a detail of the Barberini Ceiling · c. 1629–37 · National Gallery, Rome

The great creator of Baroque painting in Rome is Pietro da Cortona and the great monument of this style is the colossal ceiling frescoed by him in the palace of the Barberini during the reign of the Barberini Pope, Urban VIII. The ceiling is really an elaborate, allegorized glorification of Urban, through whom Divine Providence is shown achieving its end. It was begun in 1633 and not completed until six years later. It shows evil being overcome everywhere and the aims of the Papacy being fulfilled, but its real concern is with the power and glory of the Barberini family rather than any spiritual aim. In its general effect the ceiling is splendid to the point of confusion. It is an almost hysterical 36 assertion of glory, and aims to stun rather than to persuade.

SALVATOR ROSA (1615–73) *Mercury and the Woodman* · Oil on canvas · 49½ × 79½″ · National Gallery, London

Rosa was once one of the most famous seventeenth-century painters, particularly popular during the subsequent century for his wild, romantic scenes. He was born in Naples and worked in Rome and also in Tuscany. His fame came partly from his poetry and satires, and his lively nature, as well as from his pictures. Thundery landscapes like *Mercury and the Woodman* show how intensely he responded to the wildest poetry of nature and to the associations of lonely countryside. The figures are unimportant in this eerie scene of tangled foliage and jagged broken tree trunks, in which nature seems to grow more desolate and savage even while we gaze. It is exactly this *frisson* of the picturesque that the eighteenth century especially enjoyed.

37

MICHELANGELO CERQUOZZI (1600–1660) *The Women's Bath* · Oil
on canvas · After 1647 · Collections Marchesa Eleonora Incisa,
Rome

Cerquozzi reveals the ordinary, unpompous aspect of life and
art in seventeenth-century Rome. In addition to the creations of
classicism and the Baroque, there existed this stubborn vein of
art which resolutely concerned itself with the depictions of such
ordinary events as merrymaking and market scenes. This was
also part of the heritage from Caravaggio and, though despised
in some academic circles, it found plenty of patrons in Rome. In
fact, *The Women's Bath* cannot be a real scene but is a fantasy
perhaps inspired by some traveler's tale of the Orient. It was
owned by Cardinal Flavio Chigi, nephew of Pope Alexander VII,
and probably the most influential patron in Rome in the late
1650s. The architectural setting is by Viviano Codazzi (c. 1602–
72), who collaborated with Cerquozzi on other pictures.

Luca Giordano (1632–1705) *Apotheosis of St. Januarius* · Oil on canvas · 42 × 31¾″ · National Gallery, London

Luca Giordano is the Italian artist who bridges the Baroque and Rococo. This picture is the *modello* for a large altarpiece painted for the Neapolitans' church in Rome, showing the patron saint of Naples. All Giordano's brilliance of color, speed of execution, and vitality is compressed into it. The angel positively hurtles toward the saint, bearing the palm of his martyrdom, and everything centers on this moment of divine intervention when heaven involves itself with the affairs of man. It is exactly this sort of vision which was to be so popular with Rococo painters in the early eighteenth century.

PETER PAUL RUBENS (1577–1640) *The Judgment of Paris* · Oil on panel · $57\frac{1}{8} \times 76\frac{3}{8}''$ · National Gallery, London

Rubens is the first great Northerner of the seventeenth century to return from Italy and create a new style built on what he had learned there. Yet his art remains profoundly Flemish. *The Judgment of Paris* is a Greek story retold in the setting of Flanders. The goddesses themselves are not classically beautiful, but opulent bourgeoises of ample charm. Rubens treats the whole thing with a hint of humor—like Juno's peacock hissing at the dog crouched between the legs of Paris who has awarded the golden apple to Venus. Actually, Juno as painted by Rubens really deserves to win it, for her pose is marvelous, as in the painting 40 of her flesh set off by the crimson furred cloak.

PETER PAUL RUBENS *Marie de' Medici* · 1622–25 · Oil on canvas · $51\frac{1}{4} \times 42\frac{1}{2}''$ · The Prado, Madrid

For Marie de' Medici Rubens painted the great series of pictures of her life allegorized, and he also painted her portrait. There is nothing allegorized or high-flown about this direct portrayal, which does not disguise the Queen's plump silliness. Yet, without flattery, Rubens invests her with great dignity—emphasized by the plain setting and unadorned black dress. There is something assured about the sitter's pose and the great sweep of crisp ruff which frames her face. Indeed, the ruff is really the secret of the picture: a fan of half-transparent linen which by its sheer size imposes itself as a design over the whole picture area.

PETER PAUL RUBENS *Le Coup de Lance (Christ on the Cross)* ·
c. 1620 · Oil on canvas · 122⅛ × 68½″ · Royal Museum of Fine
Arts, Antwerp

Rubens' full maturity is represented by the famous *Coup de Lance*,
the emotional impact of which is strengthened by its huge size.
The moment chosen is at once brutal and poignant: the Virgin
virtually faints away as Longinus, the centurion, pierces Christ's
side in a tremendous gesture of force. Nothing in the composition
is at rest except the slack body of the crucified Christ. About him
twist the thieves, his grieving followers, the pawing horses—
42 contrasting with the absolute and hopeless repose of death.

PETER PAUL RUBENS *Rape of the Daughters of Leucippus* · c. 1615–16 · Oil on canvas · $87\frac{1}{2} \times 82\frac{1}{4}''$ · Alte Pinakothek, Munich

Although Rubens painted so many altarpieces and religious pictures, he was perhaps more at ease in a classical pagan world where his own sheer delight in life could find its most lyrical expression. The exuberance of this rape communicates itself to the excited horses and even to the sunny landscape. The daughters of Leucippus are almost too splendidly robust in their distress and are giving their captors a great deal of trouble. Rubens responds delightedly to the expanses of blonde flesh, set off against the brown skins of the men and made more creamy still by the glowing draperies of gold and crimson. The picture is decoration but it is dynamic decoration, spontaneous for all its large scale. 43

PETER PAUL RUBENS *Hélène Fourment and Her Children* · Oil on panel · 44½ × 32¼″ · The Louvre, Paris

Rubens' first wife died in 1626 and three years later he married a girl of sixteen, Hélène Fourment, who became the inspiration of much of his late work. The present picture is a masterpiece, intimate, tender without sentimentality, and painted with indescribable vividness. Apart from the red chair, there is no strong color in the picture—and this would probably have remained so even if it had been finished. In most ways it *is* finished, for Rubens' rapid grasp on reality is sufficient for us to complete mentally what he has only hastily sketched in—like the lower part of the chair.

PETER PAUL RUBENS *Landscape with a Tower* · 1635 · Oil on canvas · 11 × 14¾″ · Ashmolean Museum, Oxford

Religious pictures, mythologies, portraits—these did not exhaust the range of Rubens' genius. Himself the owner of a country house, the Château of Steen, he became a painter also of landscapes. In fact he had probably always responded to the atmospheric possibilities of landscape painting ever since his early years in Italy when he had known and greatly admired Elsheimer. His own landscapes are sometimes large panoramic views; sometimes, as here, they are more simple and direct, and on a smaller scale. The tradition of landscape painting was not new in northern Europe and Rubens had a great predecessor in Pieter Bruegel the Elder. But Rubens is more than an observer of nature: his response is almost empathy, and in his pictures all nature seems invested with that vitality which positively breathes from everything—animate or inanimate—that he painted.

45

ANTHONY VAN DYCK (1599–1641) *Henrietta Maria with Her Dwarf* · c. 1633 · Oil on canvas · 86¼ × 53⅜″ · National Gallery of Art, Washington, D.C.

Van Dyck is always associated with the English court of Charles I. Charles and Henrietta gave Van Dyck some of his finest opportunities, and he repaid them by a splendid series of portraits. The graceful dissembling quality of his art is well conveyed in this full-length painting of the Queen with her dwarf, Sir Geoffrey Hudson. For all its suggestion of relaxation and outdoor ease, the portrait manages to remind us casually that the sitter is royal—the crown obtrudes on the rich folds of curtain at the right.

46

ANTHONY VAN DYCK *Maria de Raet* (detail) · Oil on canvas ·
$83\frac{3}{4} \times 47\frac{3}{4}''$ · The Wallace Collection, London

Van Dyck's own nervous sensibility is reflected in this picture
with its almost disturbed painting of the elaborate lace collar and
the foaming agitated frills at Maria de Raet's wrists. She holds
with long elegant hands a feathery fan, painted with the same
nervous energy as the curls of her blond hair. The portrait has a
restless and melancholy air which is perhaps partly Van Dyck's
own. Everything is refined where Rubens would have made it
robust. Although Van Dyck was Rubens' greatest pupil, the two
men were very different artists. 47

ANTHONY VAN DYCK *Charles II of England as a Boy* · Detail from
The Children of Charles I · 1635 · Oil on canvas · 59⅜ × 60⅝″ ·
Sabauda Gallery, Turin

The complete composition shows Prince Charles (later Charles II)
at full length, standing with his brother James (later James II)
and his sister Mary. They were the three eldest children of
Charles I and the picture was painted in 1635, when Prince
Charles was five years old, for the royal court of Savoy at Turin
(where the picture has remained). Van Dyck has beautifully
solved the problem of combining childhood and royalty; the
young prince is already isolated by his importance, as heir to the
throne, but given a pet dog to rest his hand on. His clothes,
despite their richness, reveal his babyhood. He still wears long
skirts instead of breeches, and it is known that Charles I was
angry with Van Dyck for painting him in this childish costume.
Another portrait of the three children was executed in the same
year and in this Prince Charles wears adult clothes.

ANTHONY VAN DYCK *William, Prince of Orange, and Princess Mary of England* · Oil on canvas · 41¼ × 55⅞″ · Rijksmuseum, Amsterdam

This double portrait celebrates the betrothal in 1641 of Charles I's ten-year-old daughter to the young Prince of Orange. The event took place in London and at the same time the Prince gave his bride the large diamond brooch which she is seen wearing in the picture. Their son was destined to become William III of England. Once again Van Dyck solves the problem of combining dignity with informality: the embroidered silken clothes and solemn poses only emphasize the sitters' rather pathetic youth. They seem to look out of the picture with rather uncertain gaze, conscious of their importance but still timid. Van Dyck seizes the opportunity to heighten the decorative effect by recording every gleam of satin, and by contrasting the effect of the Prince's red-and-gold dress with his bride's cool green one. A few months after completing the picture, Van Dyck was dead.

JACOB JORDAENS (1593–1678) *The Painter's Family* · Oil on canvas · 71¼ × 73⅝″ · The Prado, Madrid

Jacob Jordaens was Rubens' most distinguished pupil after Van Dyck. The boisterous Baroque side of his master's art was developed by him in pictures which are rarely as sensitive and as attractive as this group portrait. Jordaens was able to capture the straightforward aspect of reality, without any of the psychological nuances of Van Dyck. Here he manages to solve the difficulty of organizing a group portrait so that it appears spontaneous and yet not awkward. Although all the sitters look out at the spectator—as if looking at a camera—they also fuse together to suggest a charming, domestic group of the different generations.

CORNELIS DE VOS (1584–1651) *A Family Group* · 1631 · Oil on canvas · 70 × 92¼″ · Royal Museum of Fine Arts, Antwerp

Cornelis de Vos was an Antwerp portrait painter, concerned especially with the depiction of prosperous bourgeois families such as the one in this painting. It is more formal than Jacob Jordaens' *The Painter's Family* but it has its own quiet charm. De Vos stems from a tradition older than Rubens, and his sitters have none of the relaxed air and naturalness projected by that great artist. The present group would be rather stiff without the presence of the children—so much more spontaneous and un-conscious than their soberly dressed, dignified parents. De Vos had a particular rapport, it would seem, with children. His portraits of children by themselves are attractive and interesting for the sympathy which the painter feels for them. The same quality is noticeable in this portrait group.

51

DAVID TENIERS THE YOUNGER (1610–90) *Still Life* · c. 1645–50 ·
Oil on canvas · 20⅝ × 27″ · Royal Museums of Fine Arts, Brussels

David Teniers, the son of a painter and the most famous member
of a family of artists, worked at Antwerp and Brussels. He is
chiefly associated with peasant scenes in the style of Brouwer, but
was capable of painting a wide variety of subjects. The present
picture is rather unusual. It is a comparatively early work and
shows Teniers' ability to make a satisfying picture out of no more
than a few books and a globe. The tonality is deliberately sober
and restrained, but in this brownish atmosphere the heavy vol-
52 umes take on a life of their own.

Diego Velázquez (1599–1660) *Pope Innocent X* · 1650 · Oil on canvas · $55\frac{1}{8} \times 47\frac{1}{4}''$ · Doria Pamphili Gallery, Rome

Diego Velázquez became court painter to Philip IV of Spain in 1623 and served the king until his death in 1660. In all those years he was permitted to leave Spain only twice, and both times he visited Italy. On the second visit he was in Rome in 1650, where he painted this portrait of the Pope—a portrait instantly famous and ever since admired. By this date Velázquez' mastery was supreme. The splendid whites and crimsons of the costume only serve to set off the flushed, almost angry, saturnine features of the Pope. Contemporaries found him difficult to fathom, but Velázquez seems to have probed to his very heart.

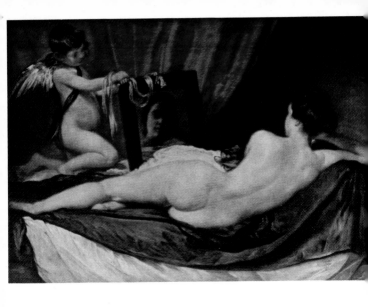

Diego Velázquez *The Rokeby Venus* · Oil on canvas · 48¼ × 69¾″ · National Gallery, London

Velázquez takes his place among the very greatest painters not just of the seventeenth century, but of all time. Few painters have achieved anything approaching his dispassionate realism, in which everything seems to obey an inevitable law and where gravity (in every sense of the word) reigns supreme. Although he painted several mythological pictures, and other nudes, *The Rokeby Venus* is his only surviving painting of a female nude. Venus is hardly a classical goddess here, but simply a woman lying on a bed. Only the winged Cupid suggests a mythological note. The picture is quite unsensual, almost unsensuous, in the simplified form of the woman's body and the very restrained coloring. It is not so much a homage to Venetian art and Titian (so splendidly represented in the Spanish royal collection) as a puritanical reworking of a Venetian theme.

Diego Velázquez *Sebastian de Morra* · c. 1643–44 · Oil on canvas · 41¾ × 31⅞″ · The Prado, Madrid

The Spanish court lives most memorably, and horribly, in the series of portraits painted by Velázquez of the dwarfs who served as objects of ridicule and humor for the royal family. Velázquez treats them with great dignity, and even perhaps with compassion. Unlike some of the other pitiful creatures painted by him, De Morra does not appear mentally afflicted. Only his pose on the ground, and the stunted legs, betray that he is a dwarf. The head has a directness of gaze which scrutinizes the spectator with great penetration. It is the humanity of this dwarf that gives a noble impact to the portrait; and the picture is also a tribute to Velázquez' humanity.

Diego Velázquez *The Surrender of Breda* · Finished 1635 · Oil on
canvas · 121⅛ × 144¾″ · The Prado, Madrid

The scene represented took place in 1625, when the Dutch city
of Breda was surrendered up by Justin of Nassau to the Spanish
General Spinola. Velázquez did not, of course, witness this
scene; he painted his picture about ten years later. It was one of
a series of battle pictures by different artists commissioned for a
hall in the palace of Buen Retiro at Madrid. Velázquez' famous
picture is very different in conception, as well as technique, from
the other pictures. It makes the Spanish victory no triumphant
moment over a humiliated enemy. The two generals meet almost
like host and guest. War is seen not as splendid, but as a tiring
struggle, and both parties seem glad it is concluded. Thus, to the
plastic realism of the painting, Velázquez adds a psychological
realism that makes the picture poignant.

Diego Velázquez *Prince Baltasar Carlos* · c. 1634 · Oil on canvas · $82\frac{1}{4} \times 68\frac{1}{8}''$ · The Prado, Madrid

There is a certain pathos in this grandiose equestrian portrait of a boy—hardly more than six years old when this picture was executed. All the hopes of his father, and Spain, were concentrated on him, but his pale, unformed face seems doomed. Since the picture was to hang high, Velázquez has painted the pony with an almost exaggerated curve of belly. Treated with full Baroque swagger, this is probably the first equestrian portrait of a child.

57

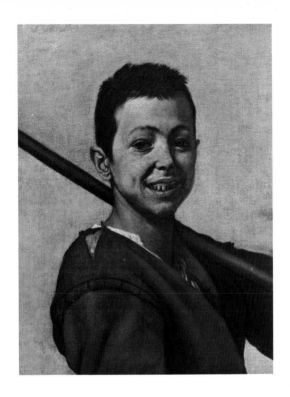

JUSEPE RIBERA (1591–1652) *Boy with a Club Foot* (detail) · 1652 ·
Oil on canvas · 64⅝ × 36¼" · The Louvre, Paris

Although born in Spain, Jusepe Ribera worked in the Spanish-
dominated city of Naples. From him derives the whole Neapolitan School of tenebrist painting, with its emphasis on dramatic
chiaroscuro and its strongly individualized saints and beggars.
Boy with a Club Foot is typical of Ribera's harsh realism, more
pungent than Caravaggio's, rougher in handling than Velázquez'.
There is even something grotesque about the boy's head, and
perhaps Ribera intended to shock by the honesty of his portrayal
of a boy both poor and deformed.

Francisco de Zurbarán (1598–1664) *St. Jerome with St. Paula and St. Eustochia* · Oil on canvas · $96\frac{1}{2} \times 68\frac{1}{8}''$ · National Gallery of Art, Washington, D.C.

Francisco de Zurbarán worked in Madrid but more especially in Seville, and represents a withdrawn private world of austere compositions and clear hand coloring. He is at his best in depicting events in the lives of the saints, not as miraculous and visionary, but as moments of such intensity that they take on a suprareality. The three figures here have all the firmness and clarity of statues carved from wood and then boldly but austerely colored. Their clothes fall with few folds; their faces are simple forms; and there is hardly any movement.

FRANCISCO DE ZURBARÁN *St. Dorothy* · c. 1645–50 · Provincial
Museum, Seville

Zurbarán painted several pictures of single female saints wearing
the ordinary Spanish clothes of the seventeenth century and
having about them an almost rustic charm. *St. Dorothy* has little
of the obviously saintly in her appearance, but Zurbarán gives
her that meditative air which marks out so much of his art. His
gift for highly original color is revealed in the juxtaposition of
the striped yellow-and-black scarf to the plum-colored dress with
its thick, heavy folds—contrasting with the wispy black veil that
floats from the saint's head. Finally, there is an intensely satisfying weight given to the beautiful still life of fruit.

Francisco de Zurbarán *Still Life of Fruit* · c. 1633 · Oil on
canvas · 23⅝ × 42⅛″ · Collection Contini Bonacossi, Florence

What had been merely an accessory in Zurbarán's *St. Dorothy*
becomes here the whole subject of a picture, recalling the still
life painted more than thirty years before by Caravaggio (see
page 25). There is something almost naïve in Zurbarán's study:
yet, at the same time, it has a tremendous conviction and an
almost mystical intensity. It is as if by concentrating on these
few carefully arranged objects the painter has discovered something about the nature of reality. What he paints is completely
free of the trivial. Three sets of objects are placed with geometrical precision in relation to each other and to the spectator;
scrupulously recorded, they seem to tell us something not only
about their external appearance, but also about their inward
essence.

BARTOLOMÉ ESTEBÁN MURILLO (1617–82) *Madonna and Child* ·
c. 1670 · Oil on canvas · 65¼ × 45¼″ · State Picture Gallery,
Dresden

Bartolomé Estebán Murillo, the third great seventeenth-century
Spanish painter, is very much less powerful and intense than
either Velázquez or Zurbarán. He is more interested in feelings,
even to the point of sentimentality. The actual paint is softer in
its application, laid on with a graceful feathery touch which—
allied to his pale vaporous coloring—makes him already a
Rococo artist. He is particularly the painter of gentle religious
pictures, obvious devotional images like this *Madonna and Child*
which is attractive, pious, but rather empty out of religious
62 context.

Bartolomé Esteban Murillo *Beggar Boys Playing Dice* · Oil on canvas · $58\frac{3}{4} \times 43\frac{1}{4}''$ · Alte Pinakothek, Munich

Murillo could not escape the genre interest of his century, an interest particularly strong in Spain. The contrast there between the showy splendor of the nobility and the desperate poverty of the ordinary people was also particularly strong. Murillo's beggar boys are poor and ragged enough, but their poverty seems invested with a certain sentimentality. They themselves are well-washed children, shown as appealing, contented gamins. Murillo's tendency to glamorize reality makes these pictures now rather difficult to appreciate, but for a long time they represented one of the most popular aspects of his art.

BARTOLOMÉ ESTEBÁN MURILLO *St. Diego* · Detail from *The "Angel-Kitchen" of St. Diego of Alcalá* · c. 1645 · Oil on canvas · $70\frac{7}{8} \times 177\frac{1}{8}''$ · The Louvre, Paris

Murillo's early work shows a stronger fiber than his later pictures. Though religious subjects are already his chief output they are treated with Ribera-like realism, as this head of St. Diego reveals. *The "Angel-Kitchen"* was painted for the Franciscans in Murillo's home town of Seville and shows the Franciscan lay brother St. Diego—the humblest of men—raised in ecstatic prayer while his kitchenwork is being done for him by angels. Harsh and unidealized, he represents that pungent actuality which is at the root of all Spanish seventeenth-century painting.

Simon Vouet (1590–1649) *Wealth* · Oil on canvas · 66⅞ × 48⅞″ ·
The Louvre, Paris

Simon Vouet stands for the most courtly, decorative side of art
in France under Louis XIII. *Wealth* is a fine example of his fluent
allegorizing and graceful painting, in which the mood is seldom
particularly serious. The very subject suits Vouet in its suggestions of prodigality, its elaborate vases and jeweled chains. But
under all this are reminders that Vouet had worked in Italy as a
young man and been influenced by Caravaggio; it is easy too to
see some influence of Gentileschi, who had worked in France. 65

NICOLAS POUSSIN (1593/4–1665) *The Lamentation of Christ* · Oil on canvas · 41 × 59⅜″ · Alte Pinakothek, Munich

Nicolas Poussin is perhaps the key figure for appreciating the oscillation of the seventeenth century between Venice and Rome, between Baroque and classicism, between *colore* and *disegno*. Though French by birth, he was Roman by adoption, and it was in Rome that he finally achieved that synthesis of opposing tendencies that is his art. *The Lamentation* is a comparatively early picture which still possesses some wild Venetian poetry. Grief is a cry of pain, as St. John sits in rigid agony and the Virgin swoons over the extended corpse of Christ. At the same period Poussin painted in similar pose the dead Adonis, mourned by Venus. The two worlds of religion and mythology remain symbolically close for him.

66

NICOLAS POUSSIN *Bacchanalian Revel before a Term of Pan* · Oil on canvas · 39¼ × 56½″ · National Gallery, London

Poussin's response to classical antiquity was intense, to the point where it could be said to be more Romantic than classical in its feeling. Gradually, however, he curbed the more spontaneous aspects of his art, organizing it with almost mathematical precision. This order has its own poetry, the poetry of harmony. In *Bacchanalian Revel* the figures are all carefully related to each other, so that the eye is led in and out of the dance. The most elaborate and beautiful pattern is formed by the left-hand trio whose arms are entwined in a way that is calculated and yet seems spontaneous. This chain of nymphs and satyrs is like a classical frieze that has come to life. Wine and blood have brought vivacity to these marble forms, and they dance gaily in a Titianesque landscape of heavy-foliaged trees.

Nicolas Poussin *The Holy Family on the Steps* · 1648 · Oil on canvas · 27 × 38½″ · National Gallery of Art, Washington, D.C. (The Samuel H. Kress Collection)

The Holy Family on the Steps was painted in 1648, at the very period when Poussin's art was reaching its richest maturity. The year before, his future biographer, André Félibien, had arrived in Rome and begun to know Poussin. In 1648 he records listening to the painter who spoke of the importance of the intellect in art, and the value of reflecting about the subject rather than directly imitating nature. This solemn *Holy Family* might have been painted to illustrate Poussin's ideas. The group forms an equilateral triangle, with its base the long line of the first step. Formalized, almost Cubist architecture rises behind—obviously an idealized construction. A few calm verticals mark off the intervals across the composition which is bathed in light and given a sense of infinity by the staircase which leads straight into the cloudy sky.

NICOLAS POUSSIN *Summer* (detail) · 1660–64 · Oil on canvas · 46½ × 63″ · The Louvre, Paris

This picture is one of the *Four Seasons* painted by Poussin for the Duc de Richelieu, begun in 1660 and finished only two years before Poussin's death. Each season is also a scene from the Old Testament. *Summer* is thus Ruth and Boaz in the cornfield, symbolizing the world since Christianity, with the marriage of Ruth and Boaz standing for the mystic marriage of Christ and the church. These layers of meaning are typical of the complexity of Poussin's very late pictures. At the same time Poussin was able to develop such symbolism without any diminution of his artistry. Even the detail of the landscape background in *Summer* is sufficient to show how responsive he remained to Italian scenery. Across the cornfield the eye is led along the winding road, to rest on the beautiful blue mountain range that lies along the horizon.

Claude Lorrain (1600–1682) *Acis and Galatea* · Oil on canvas · $39\frac{3}{8} \times 53\frac{1}{8}''$ · State Picture Gallery, Dresden

Claude Lorrain lived most of his life in Rome, like Poussin—with whom he was friendly. Passionately attached as Claude was to Italy, it was less its classical past than its romantic suggestions which formed the essence of his art. He chose to restrict himself to landscape, observed atmospherically and constructed by him on his own principle of *coulisses* and melting distances where sky and water merge. All Claude's pictures approximate dreams: dreams of a world which never was, where people have hardly any significance, where there is always mellow light and few seasonal changes. Above all, there is no hint of winter weather. *Acis and Galatea* captures the lyrical freshness of sunlight over the wide sea while the fond lovers embrace in the foreground.

CLAUDE LORRAIN *Embarkation of St. Ursula* · 1646 · Oil on canvas · 44½ × 58½″ · National Gallery, London

It was particularly during the decade of the 1640s that Claude devised a whole series of seaport scenes. Sometimes it is simply a seaport without classical or religious subject; sometimes (as in this picture of 1646) there is a definite subject, but hardly more than an excuse to animate the cloud-capped architecture. No seaport was ever like Claude's imagined scene, where water laps gently against the splendid stone steps that descend from fantastic marble palaces. Early morning light is dissolving the mist, and the ships that are to carry St. Ursula and her virgin companions float like phantoms in the liquid atmosphere.

CLAUDE LORRAIN *Landscape with the Marriage of Isaac and Rebecca* ·
1648 · Oil on canvas · 58¾ × 77½″ · National Gallery, London

Once again, the "subject" is really unimportant for Claude. His
dancing figures might be ordinary country people rather than
illustrations of an incident in the Old Testament; and the setting
is again Italy. It is a perfect pastoral scene in which ground and
trees and water have all been disposed to make a landscape more
ideal than any in fact. The trees are grouped at either side of the
composition, leaving the center for the action and also for the
suggestion of depth. Just enough interest is provided by the
figures, and then the land breaks into the large, limpid stretch of
lake which reflects the calm sky above. In Claude the landscape
interest already expressed at Rome by Elsheimer in the first
decade of the century reaches its fullest and most sophisticated
72 development.

LOUIS LE NAIN (c. 1593–1648) *The Cart* · 1641 · Oil on canvas ·
22 × 28¼″ · The Louvre, Paris

There were three brothers Le Nain, but there can be no doubt
that the greatest was Louis. Pictures can only be ascribed to him
on grounds of quality, however, since none is individually signed
by him. *The Cart* explains the nature of the Le Nain revolution,
with its uncompromisingly humble, rustic subject and its
straightforward "Dutch" manner of depicting people and things.
There is even less attempt at storytelling than in comparable
Dutch genre, and a very powerful sense of dignity. Poverty is
not made something picturesque, still less something humorous.
The life of these peasants in their farmyard is like a rebuke to the
ostentatious court world evoked by Vouet. Already in France
there are two nations—poor and rich. Perhaps it is not too
fanciful to see in Le Nain's people the ancestors of those who
were to rise in 1789 to take revenge for years of penury. 73

GEORGES DE LA TOUR (1593–1652) *St. Joseph, the Carpenter* · Oil on canvas · 52 × 38⅜″ · The Louvre, Paris

The realism of Georges de La Tour is different from that of Le Nain, though he shares the predilection for humble life. His genre and religious scenes are very similar to each other, and his treatment must have been inspired by Caravaggio. Probably he knew nothing directly of Caravaggio's work but was influenced by Dutch followers of Caravaggio, notably Honthorst. It was probably from them that he derived his fondness for indirect or concealed lighting effects, like the dramatic single candle that illuminates St. Joseph. His art has a somewhat uncouth but impressive power and originality. St. Joseph's toil at night is more than just a pictorial device. He really is a worker, and the carpenter's tools—even the spiral of shavings—help to emphasize this point. Daily life and a Biblical subject are fused in a way that must have powerfully struck home to La Tour's provincial contemporaries.

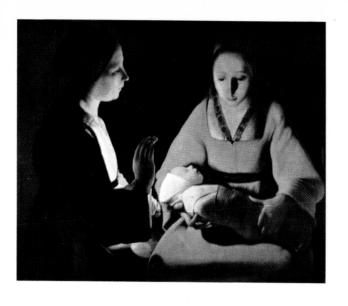

GEORGES DE LA TOUR *The Newborn Child* · Oil on canvas ·
29⅞ × 35⅞″ · Museum of Fine Arts, Rennes

In this picture La Tour achieves greater subtlety than in the
St. Joseph, and there is a more vigorous control of reality. This
time the actual candle flame is concealed and light too is more
restricted. Shadow makes the simple figures look like forms of
varnished wood, almost recalling the figures of Zurbarán, and
perhaps the two painters have something in common in their
grave and dignified realism. La Tour has restricted his colors
here, making the woman holding the candle merge into the dark
background, so that it is the warm vermilion of the mother which
attracts the eye. Mystery hovers round the composition and even
around the subject, for it may or may not represent Christ's
nativity. For La Tour the birth of *a* child and of the Christ Child
became confounded. And the picture's moving power remains
the same for us, whichever subject is intended. 75

PHILIPPE DE CHAMPAIGNE (1602–74) *Omar Talon* · Oil on canvas · $88\frac{1}{2} \times 63\frac{5}{8}''$ · National Gallery of Art, Washington, D.C. (The Samuel H. Kress Collection)

Philippe de Champaigne was Flemish by birth although working and living in France. There is a vein of powerful Flemish-style realism in his work from the first and this emerges with an increasing intellectual austerity which gives his pictures their grave air. Although he worked for royalty and for Cardinal Richelieu, Champaigne was really a painter of the middle classes, painting for them and portraying them. His sitters are posed quietly and with dignity. There is no accompanying Baroque apparatus. Instead they are seen in their ordinary environment, studied with simple directness and painted with scrupulous attention. They remind us that seventeenth-century Paris was more a bourgeois than a royal city, and that its citizens were proud of their inde-

pendence from the court.

CHARLES LEBRUN (1619–90) *Chancellor Séguier* · Oil on canvas · 116⅛ × 137¾″ · The Louvre, Paris

Charles Lebrun represents the public triumph of the arts under Louis XIV and inspired by Colbert. Colbert was the instigator of Lebrun's success not only as painter and decorator, but as virtual dictator of all artistic enterprises at the French Court. The grandiose nature of Lebrun's decorations at Versailles represents the very opposite world from that of Champaigne. And his protector Chancellor Séguier represents the typical envious and ambitious courtier. He was to persecute the Jansenists, the very sect to which Champaigne was attracted. Lebrun's portrait shows the Chancellor in his formal robes, proceeding in state like a miniature monarch, with his attendant pages. Although the result cannot be a penetrating portrait of an individual, it remains an impressive statement of power.

HYACINTHE RIGAUD (1659–1743) *Cardinal de Bouillon* · Oil on canvas · $107\frac{7}{8} \times 85\frac{3}{8}''$ · Rigaud Museum, Perpignan

Hyacinthe Rigaud carried on the tradition of the French state portrait well into the eighteenth century. Rigaud's craftsmanship is allied to considerable feeling for the character of his sitters— particularly when they are not great personages. But he always made something exciting out of the commission for a state portrait, and here the opportunity for grandeur given by the Cardinal's robes has been seized on by Rigaud with impressive effect. The Cardinal sits very much a grand seigneur and a prince of the Church. For him, however, life was to prove less calmly elevated than art. Although he was the French ambassador to Rome, of noble blood, and doyen of the cardinals, he clashed with Louis XIV and was banished from France.

Nicolas de Largillière (1656–1746) *The Family of Louis XIV* · Oil on canvas · 50 × 63″ · The Wallace Collection, London

Nicolas de Largillière was the rival of Rigaud and is usually thought of as the painter of the middle classes. His portraits are more relaxed than the formal splendors of Rigaud. Largillière has something more Flemish and direct in his depictions, even of the royal family. In this picture—which contains the king and his male heirs—there is a domestic mood, despite the grand setting in which the four generations are gathered. Largillière records their features without flattery and concentrates on the details of costume and furnishing to enliven the scene. Attention focuses finally on the child in leading strings who is the future Louis XV. 79

REMBRANDT VAN RIJN (1606–69) *Titus Reading* · c. 1656 · Oil on canvas · 27⅞ × 24¼″ · Kunsthistorisches Museum, Vienna

Rembrandt shares with Rubens the revolution whereby painting came to depict the more personal aspects of the painter: his own home and his family. While Rubens' depictions of such intimate scenes are glowing tributes to vitality, with healthy children and handsome wives, Rembrandt's are necessarily less joyful and exuberant after the first triumph of his marriage to Saskia. Their only surviving child was Titus, who was born in 1641 and lost his mother the subsequent year. There is great tenderness, as well as intimacy, in Rembrandt's portrait of his son here, painted about 1656. The artist's style had become a perfect instrument for sympathetic response to personality and atmosphere. A smoky twilight is brushed on to the canvas and out of it emerges only the sitter's face—itself absorbed—and the single hand holding the book. It is this very simplicity which makes such an impressive

picture.

REMBRANDT VAN RIJN *Danaë* · 1636 · Oil on canvas · 73 × 79″ ·
The Hermitage, Leningrad

Painted in 1636, the so-called *Danaë* is a picture which probably
represents another scene from mythology, but one with the same
type of incident of Jupiter's love for a mortal woman. The subject
is most likely that of Semele who, misled by the deceit of Juno
disguised as her nurse, made Jupiter appear by her bed in all his
majesty—and was destroyed by the lightning and thunderbolts.
Rembrandt transforms the classical story into this depiction of a
nude woman bathed in light, her flesh set off by the sheer white
of the bed's draperies. The composition is tense from Semele's
upraised half-apprehensive hand and the direction of the two
women's gaze which suggests the god is already coming. Rembrandt has wonderfully combined the eminent sense of tragedy—
above the bed a cupid weeps—with the sensuous study of a
reclining female nude.

REMBRANDT VAN RIJN *Self-Portrait in Old Age* · Oil on canvas ·
$33\frac{7}{8} \times 27\frac{3}{4}''$ · National Gallery, London

No artist has painted himself so often as did Rembrandt. His
concept of himself continued to deepen in grasp and subtlety,
while his technique grew more daring. The present portrait must
be among the very last, painted when the artist was about sixty
but had suffered the many vicissitudes which have marked his
features. Poverty and loneliness have eaten away at him and yet
he manages to stand here simply, hands clasped, and look out
with a sort of agonized resignation. Not content with this
moving concept of himself, Rembrandt gives the actual paint almost expressionistic handling.

REMBRANDT VAN RIJN *A Woman Bathing in a Stream* (Hendrickje Stoffels?) · 1654 · Oil on panel · 24⅜ × 18½″ · National Gallery, London

The picture is dated 1654 and is very likely to represent Hendrickje Stoffels, who was living with Rembrandt during the decade of the 1650s and bore him a daughter, Cornelia. Although there is no documented portrait of Hendrickje she seems to be the model for several pictures by Rembrandt, and that model in turn has affinities with the woman of the present picture. Small in scale, and probably rapidly painted, it is a brilliant sketch. The forms are almost harshly brushed in, with quick, stablike splashes of paint to suggest the folds of the white shift. As it stands, the picture is a piece of pure genre, with no subject except a woman bathing.

REMBRANDT VAN RIJN *The Flayed Ox* · 1655 · Oil on panel ·
37 × 26½″ · The Louvre, Paris

All the tendencies of seventeenth-century art toward realism are
united in Rembrandt. Despite some early Baroque pictures, he
was from the first the great master of revolutionary naturalism,
with a preference for the life and sights of his own experience.
Everything was a legitimate subject for painting; in recognizing
this Rembrandt was a pioneer of modern art. Perhaps no painter
before him would have dared to paint such a picture as *The
Flayed Ox*. The subject remains disgusting but is transfigured by
Rembrandt's art. The animal's stripped carcass is painted with an
84 astonishing bravura and tonal range.

REMBRANDT VAN RIJN *Woman with a Pink* · 1665–69 · Oil on
canvas · 36¼ × 29¼″ · Metropolitan Museum of Art, New York

In the 1630s Rembrandt was a highly successful portrait painter
in Amsterdam and his portraits are brilliant, polished likenesses
of prosperous people. Thirty years later Rembrandt was portraying only a few sitters, and in a very different style. *Woman
with a Pink* is one of these very late pictures, painted in the last
four or five years of Rembrandt's life. In place of brilliance and
polish there is now diffusion and softness. The sitter does not
confront the spectator, but seems lost in private meditation.
Almost like a musician Rembrandt creates this mood around her,
letting the shadows absorb her, while light picks out a few jewels,
the fine pleated chemise, and the bright color of the flower which
glows against the dark background.

CAREL FABRITIUS (1622–54) *The Goldfinch* · 1654 · Oil on panel ·
$13\frac{1}{4} \times 8\frac{7}{8}''$ · Mauritshuis, The Hague

Carel Fabritius was probably the most talented artist to have
passed through Rembrandt's studio. *The Goldfinch* is not only
remarkable for its *trompe l'oeil* realism and its simplicity, but also
for the typical Fabritius device—the reverse of Rembrandt's
custom—of setting dark objects against a light background. Here
the bird and cage absorb the darkness while the rough wall
behind is bathed in light. The result is to bring the spectator un-
expectedly into contact with the composition: instead of receding,
86 the bird and cage seem to jut forward.

Jan Vermeer (1632–75) *Young Woman Standing at a Virginal* ·
Oil on canvas · 20⅜ × 17¼″ · National Gallery, London

Jan Vermeer seems to have passed his whole life in the quiet
atmosphere of Delft. His art was influenced by the Utrecht
Italianate artists and also by Carel Fabritius. But he developed
the interior as a complete category of art, preferring to reduce
the strong daylight of Fabritius into the pearly tone that light has
in this picture, where it filters coolly through the window. There
is never any drama in Vermeer's compositions, which are rather
studies in silence and intimacy. Light is always the protagonist.
It fills whole cubes of space with liquid effect. Here the girl, the
instrument, the chair are each arranged almost like abstract shapes. 87

JAN VERMEER *The Little Street at Delft* · c. 1658 · Oil on canvas ·
$21\frac{3}{8} \times 17\frac{3}{8}''$ · Rijksmuseum, Amsterdam

Occasionally Vermeer moves outside into the streets of his native
town. He is the creator of the townscape panorama of Delft (in
the Mauritshuis) and also of the intimate "close-up" scene here,
which shows the influence of Carel Fabritius. The technique is
less brash than Fabritius' and the paint has a pellucid quality as
it creates the varying textures of the street, the warm brick of the
houses, and the soft sky. With Vermeer's response to the bricks
and mortar goes his feeling for the buildings as lived-in: they are
people's houses and he is concerned not only with the architecture of Delft but with ordinary life in Delft. Yet this genre interest is beautifully controlled. The scene is at once realistic and
88 heightened; it is an ideal Delft created by the artist.

JAN VERMEER *The Painter's Studio* · c. 1665 · Oil on canvas ·
47¼ × 39⅜″ · Kunsthistorisches Museum, Vienna

Vermeer's interest in effects of light, and in all optical effects,
probably reaches its culmination in this picture. Its importance is
in its formal beauty: an almost abstract beauty of the pattern of
the black-and-white tiles, the patterned curtain, and the geometrical precision of the glittering candelabra hanging from the
beamed ceiling. The painter becomes only one more object in
the beautifully planned space.

PIETER DE HOOCH (1629–after 1684?) *Interior with Woman Holding a Glass* · Oil on canvas · 29 × 25½″ · National Gallery, London

Pieter de Hooch was not born at Delft, but many of his best pictures originate during the period he lived there—after having married a Delft woman—in the 1650s, and he has left many pictorial records of its life. This *Interior* must date from this time and probably represents a tavern scene. Like Vermeer, De Hooch is fascinated by effects of light and this is more truly the subject than the ostensible genre scene. The effect is less pearly and muted than one finds in Vermeer, but an equally complete room—showing both floor and ceiling—is modeled and given recession. The woman makes an effective dark silhouette against the pale wall and window and it is in the glass that she holds up like a prism that all the room's luminous brightness seems concentrated.

PIETER DE HOOCH *A Dutch Courtyard* · c. 1656 · Oil on canvas · 26¾ × 23⅛″ · National Gallery of Art, Washington, D.C. (Mellon Collection)

In his outdoor scenes De Hooch seems to come less close to Vermeer, and to suffer less by comparison. He is fond of open-air light effects—as in this picture—which seem to be more closely related to Carel Fabritius than to Vermeer. There is less intense concentration than in Vermeer, and perhaps more of sheer charm. The painter is particularly responsive to the texture of tiles and weathered brick, wooden shutters and fences—all bathed in strong sunlight. The mood is more convivial too, and suitably open-air. Two cavaliers enjoy the spectacle of the woman drinking wine from a tall glass, watched by the solemn figure of the child at the right. A moment of ordinary life is recorded by the artist, attached deeply to his period. In place of Vermeer's timelessness we have a sense of actuality.

PIETER JANSSENS (active after 1650) *A Woman Reading* · Oil on canvas · 30 × 23¾″ · Alte Pinakothek, Munich

Pieter Janssens shows how it was possible for the comparatively minor Dutch artist to achieve at least a single masterpiece. This picture is certainly Janssens'. Without the example of Vermeer it would not have been possible, and yet the result is something very different. Its air of tranquillity is more homely than Vermeer's. Part of the picture's charm is in the air of deep domestic intimacy which it suggests—cleverly emphasized by turning the woman away from the spectator. She sits reading in a sparsely furnished room, with its bare floor made to seem yet more bare because of the pair of shoes that stand on it, making one of the few color notes in the restricted tonality. Everything breathes simplicity, silence, preoccupation.

GERARD TERBORCH (1617–81) *The Concert* · Oil on panel · 22 ×
17⅜″ · State Museums, Berlin-Dahlem

Gerard Terborch is one of the leaders in the evolution of a new
type of genre picture in seventeenth-century Holland, under the
influence of Gabriel Metsu. The interior itself is of less importance than its inhabitants, who are usually engaged in some polite
occupation—very often, as here, in music-making. But even the
figures themselves are really of less importance than the new
insistence on the decorative effect of materials, particularly
clothes. *The Concert* is memorable, above all, for the sumptuous
colors and the varied textures of the clothes worn by the woman
in the foreground. Technically brilliant though the picture is, it
is perhaps rather slight in content, and there is an almost dan-
gerous emphasis on the merely decorative. 93

GERARD TERBORCH *Boy Picking Fleas from a Dog* · Oil on canvas,
mounted on wood · 15 × 11¼″ · Alte Pinakothek, Munich

Simple scenes of ordinary life are perhaps handled by Terborch
with more feeling than his compositions of ladies in polite
society. The simplicity of the *Boy Picking Fleas* extends to the
much quieter color range and restricted tonality. Terborch makes
very effective use of the simple elements of the composition,
giving the spectator a close-up sense of the foreground table where
the boy's hat lies, and thus bringing us into contact with the
94 whole scene.

GABRIEL METSU (1629–67) *A Man Writing a Letter* · Oil on canvas · 11 × 10¼″ · Fabre Museum, Montpellier

Gabriel Metsu was probably a pupil of Gerard Dou and was to concentrate in his later years entirely on genre subjects, remarkable for their virtuosity of handling. He settled in Amsterdam and probably the present picture dates from this, the most mature period of his career. He combines the ultimate in interior painting with artificial lighting so that, for all its quiet subject matter, the picture is a drama of light and darkness. The painter is no longer concerned with daylight, but uses the light thrown by a single candle to make of the interior something at once dusky and glowing. The soft darkness increases the sense of intimacy. One's eye is even more drawn to the tenderly painted servant girl who patiently stands waiting for the letter to be finished, than to the man seated writing. As well as the drama of light, there is also a miniature drama of humanity.

GERARD DOU (1613–75) *The Doctor* · Oil on panel · 19⅜ × 14⅝″ ·
Kunsthistorisches Museum, Vienna

Gerard Dou was as a young boy a pupil of Rembrandt, but his
art was to evolve in a very different direction: toward the creation
of small, highly finished anecdotal genre pictures which were to
have tremendous success. Dou was indeed one of the most
successful artists of the period and his reputation extended
beyond Holland. *The Doctor* is very typical, especially in the
device of seeing the interior through, as it were, a window. These
"niche" pictures were, in fact, derived from Rembrandt but
popularized by Dou. The bas-relief of children playing with a
goat, which occurs in the present composition, is a favorite motif
in Dou's paintings and seems to be copied after a lost work by
96 the famous Flemish sculptor Duquesnoy.

JAN STEEN (1626–79) *The Skittle Players* · c. 1652 · Oil on panel · $31\frac{1}{4} \times 23\frac{3}{4}''$ · National Gallery, London

Jan Steen represents the livelier, and ruder, aspects of low life in seventeenth-century Holland. His pictures are often intended to be both satirical and funny. But there are other aspects to Steen—who as a painter nearly always handled the actual medium with great delicacy. There is nothing rowdy about the beautifully painted *Skittle Players* which has something of the bloom of Vermeer. The skittle players hardly disturb the peaceful atmosphere, with the trio seated at the left enjoying repose in the garden of a country inn ("The White Swan," to judge from its signboard at the left of the picture). Steen's response to natural scenery is exquisitely shown in the glowing foliage of the tall trees which rise into a sunny sky and seem to screen the inn and its visitors from all intrusion by the outside world.

ADRIAEN BROUWER (1605/6–38) *The Card Player* · Oil on panel · 13 × 16⅞″ · Alte Pinakothek, Munich

Adriaen Brouwer is the link between low-life genre painting in Flanders and Holland. He himself was Flemish by birth and he is in some ways the inheritor of the subject matter of Bruegel. But he lived part of his short life in Holland and may even have been a pupil of Frans Hals at Haarlem. His chief subject is the inn interior, usually with peasants carousing or playing cards. The present picture is typical of his ability to combine this sort of uncouth subject matter with extremely sensitive handling of paint and nuances of color—for instance, the man in green and the crumpled tablecloth.

98

HENDRICK TERBRUGGHEN (1588?–1629) *Shepherd Playing a Flute* · c. 1621 · Oil on canvas · $27\frac{5}{8} \times 21\frac{5}{8}''$ · State Picture Gallery, Kassel

Hendrick Terbrugghen studied in Italy and is the first important Northern Caravaggist to return and settle in Holland. He concentrated on religious subjects and pastoral Arcadian figures, such as this shepherd. All his work shows a very individual interpretation of Caravaggio's manner, particularly in his color schemes and his fondness for over-lifesize studies—as here—of a half-length single figure. The picture is half realistic and half fantasy—perhaps rather a boy posing as a shepherd, and equipped also with a fancy-dress hat. Terbrugghen had brought back from Italy a bold handling and revolutionary realism which were to become established especially at Utrecht and to lead to a whole group of Caravaggesque artists there.

ADRIAEN VAN OSTADE (1610–54) *The Fiddler* · Oil on panel ·
$17\frac{5}{8} \times 16\frac{1}{2}''$ · Mauritshuis, The Hague

Adriaen van Ostade is said to have been a pupil of Brouwer and
there is great affinity of subject matter between the two painters.
Like Brouwer, he preferred to depict the life of merrymaking
peasants; and here the visit of a wandering fiddler to a village inn
provides him a subject. His pictures are usually small in scale and
he was enormously prolific and popular. A whole stream of
imitations and copies began to flow already at that period, and
his work remained in vogue—especially in France—during the
eighteenth century. 99

GERARD VAN HONTHORST (1590–1656) *The Procuress* (detail) ·
c. 1625 · Oil on panel · 28 × 41″ · Centraal Museum, Utrecht

Gerard van Honthorst was one of the principal channels for the
dissemination of Caravaggio's style in northern Europe. Probably
younger than Terbrugghen, he lived much longer and became
an internationally famous figure. He trained in Rome and was
particularly to popularize the night scene (in Italy he was called
Gherardo della notte) and highly realistic candlelight effects similar
to that in *The Procuress*, which dates from after his return to
Utrecht. The scene is a typical one of genre, but very carefully
planned—the device of the dark shape of the pleading man
silhouetted in profile at the left, which throws into vivid relief the
smiling woman, so provocatively illuminated. In this way the
dramatic contrasts of extreme light and darkness are paralleled
by the psychological drama of the subject itself.

FRANS HALS (c. 1580–1666) *The Gipsy Girl (La Bohémienne)* · Oil on panel · 22¾ × 20½″ · The Louvre, Paris

Frans Hals was Flemish by origin and was probably born at Antwerp. But early in his life his parents settled at Haarlem and Hals was to remain active there for the whole of his long career. Besides painting portraits, he was the creator of genre studies, usually of single figures as in *The Gipsy Girl*. While the subject recalls Terbrugghen and Honthorst, the striking difference is Hals's lively handling of paint—which has something of Rubens in its rapid sketchlike brilliance. In this picture the girl's white chemise is painted with dazzling broken touches, jagged strokes of paint which give the material as much vivacity as her face. Everything gives the feeling of having been seized as an "impression"—a fleeting moment as transitory as the girl's expression. The color is deliberately restricted and simple. Hals was to have many pupils and exert great influence—not least on Manet and the Impressionists in the nineteenth century.

102

FRANS HALS *Banquet of the Officers of the Guild of St. George*
(detail) · 1627 · Oil on canvas · $70\frac{1}{2} \times 101\frac{1}{4}''$ · Frans Hals
Museum, Haarlem

This detail gives a sufficient idea of the crowded group portraits
of guilds and military companies that were to be a speciality of
Hals's work. Such portraits raised problems—among them the
need to give a good likeness and equal prominence to each sitter
in the group. Hals was able to solve this by very full lighting of
the sitters and by giving an almost snapshot air of actuality to all
the varying poses. The result manages to be informal and yet
coherent, as well as dignified. The opportunities offered for color
and decorative effect were chiefly restricted to the sashes and
banners of the companies. Hals cleverly makes use of these as
the final enlivening touch to the large composition. The air of
gay improvisation is misleading because, to achieve this apparent
spontaneity, the artist had to work very hard.

Frans Hals *The Women Regents of the Haarlem Almshouse* · 1664 ·
Oil on canvas · 67¼ × 98″ · Frans Hals Museum, Haarlem

Despite his great productivity, Frans Hals suffered for many
years from financial difficulties. In his very last years he and his
wife were dependent on public charity at Haarlem and perhaps
it is no accident that in these years his art took on a new depth.
He now portrayed not gay military companies but the rather
severe-looking groups who managed the charitable institutions
of the city. *The Women Regents* was painted in 1664, not long before his death, and shows an almost Rembrandtesque profundity
in its depiction of five plainly dressed women in a very simple
setting. There is no suggestion of movement, but an intense
104 gravity in these sober faces which reflect age and wisdom.

JOHANNES VERSPRONCK (1597–1662) *A Little Girl in Blue* · Oil
on canvas · $32\frac{1}{4} \times 26\frac{1}{4}''$ · Rijksmuseum, Amsterdam

Johannes Verspronck is not a major painter, but the creator at
times of memorable portraits. He was a Haarlem artist who
studied under Frans Hals. His brushwork is less showy than that
of Hals, but he has at least equal receptivity to the character of
the sitter—and this sensitive portrait is a demonstration of it.
The child is dressed up in finery—beautifully painted white lace
and unexpected, pale blue stiff silk—but yet retains the touching
appeal of childhood. Though so simple and effective in presentation, the portrait indicates a revolution in accepting children as
subjects for pictures. The social and family side of Dutch life at
the period is summed up in this minor masterpiece.

HERCULES SEGHERS (1589/90–1633) *Landscape with the Meuse* ·
c. 1625–27 · Canvas on panel · $11\frac{1}{2} \times 18''$ · Boymans-van Beuningen Museum, Rotterdam

Hercules Seghers is an important pioneer of landscape in seventeenth-century Holland, both as a painter and etcher. There is
likely to have been an exchange of influence between him and
Rembrandt (who owned as many as eight pictures by Seghers).
Seghers represents also the transition from the Flemish fantasy
landscapes of the later sixteenth century to the more powerful
realistic seventeenth-century landscapes which were to be created
in Holland. Seghers himself retains some elements of romantic
feeling in his panoramic mountainous scenes, with thundery
effects and bold monochromatic handling. In the present picture,
the foreground is heavily shadowed, and its oppressive effect is
broken only by the gleam of distant water. The feeling of wild-
106 ness is accentuated finally by the absence of human figures.

Jacob van Ruisdael (1628/29–82) *Wheatfields* · c. 1670 · Oil on canvas · 39⅜ × 51¼″ · Metropolitan Museum of Art, New York

Jacob van Ruisdael is probably the greatest of the Dutch seventeenth-century landscape painters. As well as distinguished pupils like Hobbema, he had many pupils and imitators. Strong pride in the landscape of Holland is expressed in his work, with its response above all to the shifting patterns of light and shade in a northern country so often overcast and cloudy. Ruisdael's wunderful skies are never quite still. Indeed, he prefers the ominous atmospheric effect that broods over the wheatfields, where light turns livid the strips of the fields and the patch of road where a man walks. While the actual landscape has nothing remarkable or grand about it, the sky is an agitated pageant of streaming clouds which makes the spectator feel—almost physically—the weather depicted.

JACOB VAN RUISDAEL *The Mill near Wijk-bij-Duurstede* (detail) ·
c. 1670 · Oil on canvas · 32⅝ × 39¾″ · Rijksmuseum, Amsterdam

In Ruisdael's best pictures, the ever-changing pattern of light and
shade seems almost to mirror the artist's character, and he is
never better than when catching an oppressive, thundery atmosphere. Here the tall shape of the mill stamps itself boldly against
the overcast sky, while a patch of red roof gleams with sinister
brightness. With his sensitivity to atmosphere goes Ruisdael's
feeling for the textures of wood and foliage and stone.

PHILIPS KONINCK (1619–88) *Extensive Landscape with a Hawking Party* · Oil on canvas · $52\frac{1}{4} \times 63\frac{1}{8}''$ · National Gallery, London

Philips Koninck seems to have been influenced as a landscape painter by both Rembrandt and Seghers. Although now thought of largely as a landscape painter, Koninck in his own period was better known for his portraits and genre scenes. *Extensive Landscape* shows a vast panorama, apparently seen from a very high viewpoint. Indeed, landscape is subordinated to the vast area of cloud-filled sky where heavy cumulus lies almost threateningly over the flat countryside. The dramatically dark band of shadow that wraps the middle distance is broken by distant gleams over the town and far hills—a device recalling Segher's *Landscape with the Meuse* (page 106).

MEINDERT HOBBEMA (1638–1709) *The Avenue, Middelharnis* ·
c. 1689 · Oil on canvas · 40¾ × 55½″ · National Gallery, London

Meindert Hobbema represents a more prosaic world than Ruisdael's, though he was Ruisdael's pupil and very much indebted
to the older artist's example. *The Avenue* is Hobbema's masterpiece—a masterpiece of effectiveness which, once seen, is always
remembered. Neither the sky nor the landscape is painted with
the sensitivity of Ruisdael. Hobbema is much more the recorder
of actual topography—and this view of Middelharnis is remark-
ably accurate. But thanks to the presence of the tall trees that
line the avenue, Hobbema has a perfect subject: the eye is led for
a walk up the perspective of the narrowing road, to encounter
the man strolling with his dog. The composition is bold and
instantly memorable. Hobbema has produced a picture which is
110 the quintessential landscape of seventeenth-century Holland.

PAULUS POTTER (1625–54) *Landscape with a Boar* · 1650 · Oil on canvas · 11⅜ × 11″ · Collection Van Beuningen, Vierhouten

Paulus Potter was the son of a painter and clearly precocious during his brief lifetime. He concentrated on small pictures, almost always of animals in landscapes, painted with great care and delicate aerial effects—as in the subtly colored sky of the present landscape. Once so famous, and now rather neglected, Potter is one of those painters with the equivalent of nearly perfect pitch. There is an uncanny accuracy of tone in the warm light that here bathes the hillside with the deer and the clump of trees at the left. It is a softer and more lyrical atmosphere than that of either Ruisdael or Hobbema. An almost southern sunshine makes the whole picture glow with warmth.

ALBERT CUYP (1620–91) *A Herdsman with Cows by a River* · Oil on panel · 17⅞ × 29⅛″ · National Gallery, London

Albert Cuyp began to paint first in the style of Jan van Goyen but gradually his pictures became flooded with a golden light such as in the present view. Though the subject and setting are typically Dutch, there is an Italian warmth and brightness which Cuyp probably derived from such artists as Jan Both who had lived in Italy. With Cuyp the landscape and the cattle are hardly more than objects to diversify the buoyant atmosphere—all liquid sky and crystalline water. In this atmosphere everything is washed into soft tones of caramel and golden-brown. The figures are like corks—stubby like them, too—which seem to float between sea and sky. The elements are Cuyp's subject and in his pictures seem always calm and domestic, a fitting environment for country people going about their daily life.

Jan van Goyen (1596–1656) *Haarlemmermeer* · 1656 · Oil on canvas · 15⅝ × 27¼″ · Städel Institute, Frankfurt

Jan van Goyen was one of the most prolific of Dutch landscape painters, working all over Holland. The present picture was painted in the year of his death and shows the final evolution of his style. He is particularly the painter, not so much of Dutch landscape, as of Dutch seascape—perpetually reminding the spectator of the ever-present water that intersects and partly surrounds Holland. With Van Goyen water is a mirror of the sky. He creates stormy effects—as in the present picture—in which people and land dwindle to mere black dots and strips, and only a few boats drift somberly, their sails dark against the lurid sky with its scudding, ragged clouds.

WILLEM VAN DE VELDE (1633–1707) *The Cannon Shot* · Oil on canvas · 30⅞ × 26⅜″ · Rijksmuseum, Amsterdam

Willem van de Velde turns the seascape increasingly into a representation of shipping or of actual naval events. The present picture shows his attention to the minutiae of the structure and rigging of vessels—though no particular historic moment is depicted. The man-of-war at the right fires a cannon shot probably as a salute and this explosion alone disturbs the placed calm of the scene. Historically Van de Velde represents the rise of two great maritime empires—those of Holland and England. It is no accident that, having worked in Holland as a young man, he settled in England and found considerable employment there.

Ambrosius Bosschaert (c. 1565–1621) *Vase of Flowers* · Oil on canvas · $12\frac{5}{8} \times 10\frac{3}{8}''$ · Collection Perman, Stockholm

Ambrosius Bosschaert was Flemish by birth but was to live and work in Holland. He is one of the first painters restricting himself to the new category of the flower piece, and Flemish and Dutch styles agreeably combine in his pictures. He is fond of setting the flowers in a glass vase placed on a ledge—as here—and with a very Flemish-style landscape extending behind. The flowers themselves are painted with an almost primitive directness, which is part of the picture's charm. As well as being decorative, the picture stands for the seventeenth century's developing interest in the natural world: in botany, and even in insects and shells. All are recorded with scientific fidelity and the picture may be said to instruct as well as to please.

WILLEM KALF (1619–93) *Still Life* · 1662 · Oil on canvas ·
$25\frac{1}{4} \times 20\frac{7}{8}''$ · State Museums, Berlin-Dahlem

Willem Kalf is the Vermeer among painters of still life, with a
deep, glowing sense of color and feeling for light-bathed textures
that probably do derive from the great Delft artist. In Dutch
seventeenth-century painting, the still life becomes a category of
picture, and in Kalf the arrangement of a few objects on a table
is not so much a reflection of ordinary domestic life as a completely artistic invention. He chooses his objects very carefully:
here a Chinese bowl and lid are set off in tone by the orange and
the unpeeled lemon, and they in turn by the richly colored
Turkish rug. The light falls warmly on all these different surfaces
and Kalf achieves a sensuous effect from juxtaposing the various
textures of hard porcelain and glass, soft rug, and mat surface of
the fruits.

WILLEM CLAESZ HEDA (1593/94–1680/82) *Still Life (Breakfast Table)* · Oil on panel · 21¼ × 32¼″ · State Picture Gallery, Dresden

Willem Claesz Heda represents a more austere and cooler-toned version of the still-life picture when compared with Kalf. If Kalf is always seeking strong sunlit effects, Heda prefers almost moon-blanched tones of gray and greenish-silver. In place of Kalf's rich rug this *Still Life* shows a plain white tablecloth, with a few pewter plates. The background is Heda's typical plain one, colored very much the same as the grayish glasses of pale wine. The whole atmosphere is as if bathed by northern light. In its cold clarity Heda depicts everything with great precision and delicacy. Like Kalf, he transcends the mere recording of objects and achieves an abstract, nearly geometrical, beauty of shapes. 117

PIETER SAENREDAM (1597–1665) *Interior of the Church of Assendelft* · Oil on panel · 19⅝ × 29⅞″ · Rijksmuseum, Amsterdam

Pieter Saenredam, one of the leading painters of church interiors, was not only interested in architectural effects in pictures but was in touch with important architects of the period—such as Jacob van Campen, the builder of the Town Hall at Amsterdam. In Saenredam's drawings there is an architectural accuracy which accords well with the artist's practice of noting the actual day and month, as well as the year, when the drawing was executed. But in his paintings Saenredam is freer and can modify for compositional reasons the actual structure of a building. The result is to give a timeless quality to his blond church interiors where the eye is led serenely through a succession of arches and vaults, all honey-colored, as if into infinity.

Jan van der Heyden is more than a recorder of the urban scene in seventeenth-century Holland. He is the creator of scenes where the actual and the imaginary are blended for artistic effect. Even when his pictures seem entirely accurate topographically they are often full of slight fantasy elements which give to them an almost ideal air—the air of being perfect towns. Van der Heyden's response to light gives everything a crystal clarity: serene skies arch over luminously glowing buildings and streets. His townscapes seem as miniature and clear as if captured in a glass paperweight. There is always about them a peepshow effect, reminding one that painted peepshows were a specialty of Holland at the period.

JAN ASSELYN (1610–52) *A Roman Bridge* · Oil on canvas · 32 × 46⅛″ · Collection Duke of Bedford, Woburn Abbey, Bletchley

Jan Asselyn lived and worked for some years in Italy before settling in Holland. He was certainly influenced by the achievements of several artists in Rome, most outstandingly by Claude. It is a warmer version of Claude's light that floods his pictures— and in *A Roman Bridge* it has become a deep sunset glow that lends the final suggestion of romance to the scene. Italy is seen not so much literally as in a dreamlike haze, with all the associations of country, ruins, southern light, fused into an almost visionary whole. It is a view of Italy very consciously seen through the eyes of a Northern artist.

GIUSEPPE MARIA CRESPI (1665–1747) *Girl with a Flea* · c. 1707–9 ·
Oil on canvas · 18 × 13⅜" · Uffizi Gallery, Florence

Giuseppe Maria Crespi bridges the gap between the Bolognese
tradition of the seventeenth century and the revived Venetian
School of the eighteenth century. In Crespi there is carried on a
response to the actual medium of oil paint, as well as a Caravaggesque love of dramatic effects of light, and an intensive
realism of setting. The natural and the undignified appeal to
Crespi; he invests them with his own sense of human dignity.
Girl with a Flea is a deliberate piece of humble, even squalid,
genre. It asserts the truth of the individual and shows that art
can take any subject and make a picture out of it.

ALESSANDRO MAGNASCO (1677–1749) *Punchinello and His Son* ·
Oil on canvas · $13\frac{3}{8} \times 12\frac{1}{4}''$ · Collection Hoine Gatte Casazza,
Venice

Alessandro Magnasco is still a rather mysterious figure whose
highly personal style of painting seems the reflection of a strange,
haunted character. His rapid calligraphic handling of paint looks
forward to the Guardi, but his color is much more sober than
theirs. His elongated figures are agitated and shaken as if by
fever and the mood of his pictures is melodramatic. *Punchinello
and His Son* is in a more tender vein than is usual with Magnasco.
In place of hysterically praying monks there is only this simple
group of father and child sitting eating in a kitchen. The picture
is, in one sense, ordinary genre, but genre heightened by the
figures, which are from the *commedia dell'arte* yet are shown not
122 acting, but at a private and domestic moment.

SEBASTIANO RICCI (1659–1734) *Esther before Ahasuerus* · Oil on canvas · $18\frac{1}{2} \times 13''$ · National Gallery, London

Sebastiano Ricci was the oldest of the creators of the Rococo at Venice. He turned back to the great Venetians of the sixteenth century, particularly Veronese. Veronese's brilliant colors and superb decorative effects were to inspire Ricci to such pictures as *Esther before Ahasuerus* which is probably a late work and shows the painter at his most accomplished—but still with echoes of Veronese in design and color. It is a typically operatic, Rococo moment of drama which is shown as Esther dares to appear before Ahasuerus and the king extends in mercy toward her his golden scepter.

SEBASTIANO RICCI *The Resurrection* · Fresco · Chapel of the Royal Hospital, Chelsea

As well as working in Vienna and visiting Paris, Sebastiano Ricci traveled to England. He was tempted to go by the prospect of decorating the dome of St. Paul's, but he failed to get the commission. However, he did decorate the apse of Chelsea Hospital Chapel with *The Resurrection*. Here he revealed to English eyes a new lightness of palette and an almost gay drama even in a religious subject. His decorative gifts enabled him to solve the problem of filling the apse with an animated and effective composition. It is into a golden heaven radiant with hosts of clustering angels that Christ triumphantly rises. Everything sweeps about him and he is like the conductor of some colossal orchestra who sets the whole composition in motion.

GIOVANNI ANTONIO PELLEGRINI (1675–1741) *Musicians* · Oil on plaster · Kimbolton Castle School

Giovanni Antonio Pellegrini was the most traveled of all the peripatetic Venetian Rococo decorators and the first to come to England. For the Duke of Manchester's country house, Kimbolton, he painted several decorations including, on a staircase, the *Musicians*. The picture is painted in oils on the plaster of the wall and has a brilliance of color partly achieved by heavy impasto. As so often with these artists, the inspiration derives from Veronese who had already made marvelous use of Oriental costumes. Pellegrini treats the problem of decoration in a thoroughly lighthearted manner and with the playful piece of illusionism whereby the boy leans out of the composition to feed the dog. No story is told. Three brilliantly clad musicians enchantingly play on a feigned balcony; they and the boy are the only "subject."

GIOVANNI ANTONIO PELLEGRINI *Rebecca at the Well* · Oil on canvas · 50 × 40″ · National Gallery, London

There is a sense of improvisation about all Pellegrini's compositions, even when they have a subject such as this Biblical scene. The setting is seldom more than a feathery tree—virtually a theatrical property—and the figures too have a feathery insubstantiality as if made up from twists of colored drapery. Pellegrini simply makes the occasion an opportunity to paint one of his favorite blond women—her blondness set off by ravishing blue and white clothes—and pose her in a faintly exotic atmosphere. Above all, the picture is intended to be decoration and Pellegrini never forgets that intention. Light and air and shimmering color all go to serve his purpose and contribute to the final decorative effect.

GIAMBATTISTA TIEPOLO (1696–1770) *Temptation of St. Anthony* ·
Oil on canvas · 15¾ × 18½″ · The Brera, Milan

Giambattista Tiepolo is the culmination of all the decorative
tendencies of Venetian art, going back to Veronese and including
Ricci and Pellegrini. He is also the end of that splendid tradition.
When he died in Madrid the Rococo movement, already under
attack for several years, was over. The climate of pure imagination which he represents was being replaced by serious Neoclassic
"truth." History was replacing mythology, and the dreams and
visions devised by Tiepolo were to seem frivolous to a more
sober generation. *Temptation of St. Anthony* is an early work but it
already reveals Tiepolo's imaginative gifts. The huddled dark
figure of the saint is less important than the delightful Temptation herself, almost a hallucination.

GIAMBATTISTA TIEPOLO *The Holy House of Loreto* · Oil on canvas · $48\frac{7}{8} \times 33\frac{1}{2}''$ · Academy of Fine Arts, Venice

No surface was too huge for Tiepolo to decorate, but his decorations have much less flippancy than Pellegrini's. He believes utterly in his own art and is able to create a completely valid imaginative world where nothing is impossible. Instinctively attracted to the miraculous—to all those moments when nature's law is broken—he was able to serve the Church magnificently. For churches all over North Italy, as well as at Venice, he frescoed and painted glorious visionary moments, like this of the Holy 128 House being swept through the sky from Bethlehem to Loreto.

GIAMBATTISTA TIEPOLO *Rinaldo and Armida* · Oil on canvas ·
39¼ × 55″ · Bavarian State Galleries, Munich

Again and again Tiepolo returned to the story, told by Tasso in
Gerusalemme Liberata, of how the wicked enchantress Armida
carried off the hero Rinaldo to her magic gardens where he for-
got everything in his love for her. But the story was told in the
eighteenth century by others besides Tiepolo. It was one of those
stories of man beguiled by woman—like that of Anthony and
Cleopatra—that the century loved. It was an opera, a ballet, the
subject for numerous painters of all countries. And Tiepolo
captures all the ingredients of the story, paying his tribute too to
his century's obsession with the power of women.   129

DOMENICO TIEPOLO (1727–1804) *The Minuet* · Oil on canvas ·
$30\frac{7}{8} \times 43\frac{5}{8}''$ · Catalan Museum of Fine Arts, Barcelona

Domenico Tiepolo was the devoted collaborator of his father
whom he loyally served until the latter's death. But Domenico
himself was really a very different artist, attached not to the world
of imagination but to the solid world of fact. This appealed to
his sense of the ludicrous, the satirical, and the topical. He is at
home with clowns and mountebanks and masked dancers—
figures recognizably from the Venice of his own period, wittily
observed and set down in sparkling paint. Above all, he is linked
to the new spirit of realism which pervaded the art of Goldoni.
The dancing figures in Domenico's pictures might be characters
strayed from a Goldoni comedy.

POMPEO GIROLAMO BATONI (1708–87) *Time Destroying Beauty* ·
1746 · Oil on canvas · $53\frac{1}{4} \times 28''$ · National Gallery, London

Pompeo Girolamo Batoni stands as one of the leading exponents
of the new Neoclassic style which took root in Rome and was to
oppose successfully the Venetian Rococo. However, Batoni
did not altogether understand the Neoclassic and he was certainly
not a seriously "engaged" artist of the caliber of David, nor,
intellectually, could he equal his German contemporary, Mengs.
But his coldly sculptural art is grave and still, after the airy
movement of the Rococo. 131

GIAMBATTISTA PIAZZETTA (1683–1754) *Assumption of the Virgin* ·
1735 · Oil on canvas · 203 × 96⅞″ · The Louvre, Paris

Trained under Crespi, Giambattista Piazzetta was not naturally
sympathetic to the rainbow colors and movement of the Venetian
decorators. The son of a woodcarver, he seems always to have
been conscious of form and volume, and to prefer to model his
figures in thick paint and in deliberately restricted tones of gray
and white and brown—all used with exquisite effect. The
Assumption is one of his largest altarpieces and was painted in
1735 for the Archbishop-Elector of Cologne, a great patron of
132 Venetian artists.

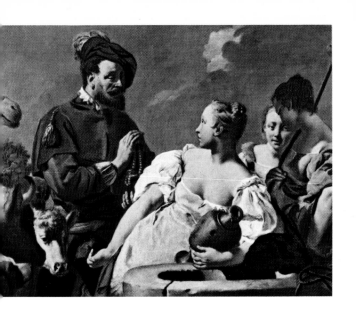

GIAMBATTISTA PIAZZETTA *Rebecca at the Well* · Oil on canvas ·
40⅛ × 53⅞″ · The Brera, Milan

The contrast with Pellegrini's treatment of the same theme (page
126) tells something about the individuality of Piazzetta's art in
the Venice of his day. Unlike Pellegrini and Tiepolo, Piazzetta
was a slow worker. He was a rather withdrawn personality,
though a teacher with many pupils. There is in his *Rebecca* a sense
of drama that Pellegrini's completely lacks. Rebecca is a peasant
girl surprised by the advances of a well-dressed, dashing gentleman
who dangles a pearl necklace to attract her. Two rather sly
girls at the right seem to be quite amused by the situation, and
the whole picture breathes an unexpected air of countrified
humor. The scene is treated not in terms of dignity, or charm,
but in terms of plain humanity.

PIETRO LONGHI (1702–85) *The Dancing Lesson* (detail) · Oil on canvas · 23⅝ × 19¼″ · Academy of Fine Arts, Venice

Pietro Longhi was to satisfy the interest of his century in ordinary humanity by painting small pictures of prosperous life as it was lived behind the façades of Venetian palaces. He is the devoted recorder of the daily existence there—and nowhere else. His people are usually engaged in amusing themselves, but the sentiments expressed are always very tentative. A man and woman may dance decorously—as here—watched by the fiddler and chaperoned by another woman. As documents of the life of the day, Longhi's pictures have a prettiness and charm which 134 does not always avoid the trivial.

PIETRO LONGHI *The Rhinoceros* · 1751 · Oil on canvas · 23⅞ × 19⅛″ · Rezzonico Palace, Venice

The coming of a rhinoceros to Venice, for the carnival of 1751, created a great stir and a demand for paintings of the animal. Longhi's picture is a record of it, done—as the inscription tells—for the patrician Giovanni Grimani. It is quite likely that Grimani is the man standing in the center of the composition, between the showman and the woman in carnival dress. A certain blankness in the spectators' reaction to the rhinoceros seems part of a curious vacuity in Longhi himself. He seldom bothers to organize his picture properly and convinces us more by his attention to detail than by his powers of composition. But he is part of Venice's obsession with itself in the last years of the Republic when its power had dwindled and it had become a show place.

ANTONIO CANALETTO (1697–1768) *Ascension Day at Venice* · Oil on canvas · 71⅝ × 102″ · The Crespi Collection, Milan

Antonio Canaletto did not invent the view picture *veduta*, but with him it became a new and quite definite category of picture. Its popularity and his fame resulted in a host of imitators and followers who fed on the picturesqueness of Venice. Venice is the subject of much of Canaletto's best work. Here the city is seen in the most splendid and important of all its festivals—that of Ascension Day, when the Doge rowed across the Lagoon for the Wedding of the Sea, symbolized by a ring dropped into the waters of the Adriatic. Canaletto not only conveys the bustling scene in the Bacino before the Doge's Palace but also responds to the whole atmosphere with passages of marvelous painting which suggest the water, the boats, the hangings, and finally the calm shapes of the buildings that are quintessentially Venice.

ANTONIO CANALETTO *View of the Thames* (detail) · Private collection, London

Canaletto was from the first much patronized by English visitors to Venice and it was probably inevitable that he should finally come to England. With brief visits back to Venice, he spent about ten years in England after 1746, painting one or two other places but concentrating on London. The Thames offered him the best substitute for his native city's Grand Canal and he seems to have preferred rather distant views which allowed him to present a panorama of London and the river. English light did not have the sparkle of Venetian, and the architecture in London clearly did not appeal very much to him. But water and boats and bridges could still be painted with the detail, and affection, that came from Canaletto's knowledge.

BERNARDO BELLOTTO (1720–80) *View of the Gazzada* · 1744 · Oil
on canvas · 25⅝ × 39¼″ · The Brera, Milan

Bernardo Bellotto was the pupil of his uncle, Canaletto, and his
early work betrays the debt. But Bellotto was basically a rather
different painter, though he continued the tradition of the view
picture. When quite young he left Italy forever, and painted at
Dresden, Vienna, and—eventually—Warsaw, where he settled.
View of the Gazzada is one of his rare early paintings of an
Italian scene, but already the tonality is distinct from Canaletto's,
as is the technique. Cool shades of blue and green give an almost
subaqueous effect to Bellotto's pictures and he seems to have
more affinity with northern than with southern light—even in
138 his early work.

FRANCESCO GUARDI (1712–93) *Ascension Day at Venice* · Oil on canvas · 26¼ × 39½″ · The Louvre, Paris

Francesco Guardi is inevitably compared with his contemporary Canaletto, by whom he was certainly influenced. Although this picture represents a different moment from that in Canaletto's picture (page 136), together they make a fascinating comparison and neatly reveal how very diverse was the two painters' attitude to depicting the Venetian festival. Guardi's is a much more airy scene, more loosely composed and more impressionistic in handling. Everything is subordinated to the almost equal expanses of sea and sky. Between these two elements the boats seem frail structures, and people dwindle to being hardly bigger than ants. Buildings are pushed well away into the distance. And sparkling light blends water and air into one atmospheric whole. 139

Francesco Guardi *Venice: The Doge's Palace* · Oil on canvas ·
22¾ × 30″ · National Gallery, London

The miracle of Venice remains its rising from the waters of the
Lagoon—a sight that can never fail to surprise and enchant.
Guardi seems always moved by it, always responsive to the
ubiquitous water which laps at the base of the buildings and
makes them all become like boats. His view of the Doge's
Palace and the buildings along the Molo emphasizes the jumbled
effect, and the straggling line of buildings receding into the
distance. It is a different truth from Canaletto's, more wayward
and perhaps more poetic. Guardi is the last great interpreter of
the city. And four years after his death the Republic came to
an end.

Francesco Guardi *Venice: Piazza San Marco* · Oil on canvas ·
$11\frac{5}{8} \times 17\frac{3}{4}''$ · Kunsthistorisches Museum, Vienna

In his late work Guardi is completely emancipated from Canaletto. His style has become the complete expression of his artistic
personality and it is well summed up in the present picture.
Even the architecture of Piazza San Marco seems to have changed,
because Guardi shows the Piazza with the elaborate wooden
arcading designed by Macaruzzi in 1776 and from that time on
erected in the Piazza during the Ascension Day carnival. This
graceful structure breaks the familiar rectangle of the scene, and
Guardi enjoys the sweeping curves which have a Rococo vivacity.
The same vivacity animates the tiny figures which are mere
squiggles and drops of paint and which yet communicate a lively
sense of life.

FRANCESCO GUARDI *Venice: Piazza San Marco* (detail) · Oil on canvas · 24 × 39″ · Carrara Academy, Bergamo

Where Canaletto recorded Venice with precision, asserting the firm verticals and horizontals of its edifices, Guardi exaggerates the drama of the city. His *Piazza San Marco* is seen in steep perspective, with the campanile of San Marco rising tall and needle-thin—taller and thinner than in Canaletto's views, but the drama and shade here remind one of Canaletto's early pictures. From him Guardi has borrowed the effective device of plunging the Procuratie buildings at the right into deep shadow and then showing the patch of Doge's Palace beyond bathed in warm sunlight.

Franz Anton Maulpertsch (1724–96) *The Holy Family* · Oil
on canvas · 50 × 33⅜″ · Kunsthistorisches Museum, Vienna

Franz Anton Maulpertsch is only one of the great Rococo
painters produced in Austria and Germany during the eighteenth
century. It could be said that the Rococo was really most at home
there, and certainly nowhere else were buildings so beautifully
designed to accommodate altarpieces and frescoes. The tendency
toward dissolution of forms is shown at its most extreme in the
sweet mists of bright color which drift across Maulpertsch's
pictures. The figures pose with affected grace, gesticulating with
elegant, fluid hands, all reminiscent of Bavarian Rococo sculp-
ture.

ANTOINE WATTEAU (1684–1721) *The Judgment of Paris* · 1720 ·
Oil on canvas · 18½ × 12¼″ · The Louvre, Paris

Antoine Watteau does more than represent the emancipation of
French art from officialdom in the early eighteenth century. He
stands for the completely personal mood in art—as much as
Giorgione, if not more—and for a typically eighteenth-century
interest in the psychology of love. Virtually a Fleming by birth,
he had a native affinity to Rubens, whose health and vigor he
must have envied. He himself was, in handling of paint, a Rubens
turned miniaturist. It is significant that *The Judgment of Paris* was
a subject painted several times by Rubens (see page 40), and
Watteau's composition if full of reminiscences of Rubens. But
Watteau's scene is much more intimate.

ANTOINE WATTEAU *Fête Vénitienne* (detail) · 1718/19 · Oil on canvas · 22 × 18″ · National Gallery of Scotland, Edinburgh

This detail shows the central figure, the woman dancing in a park, in the so-called *Fête Vénitienne*. It probably dates from late in Watteau's brief career, when his wonderfully sensitive handling of textures had reached the pitch revealed by the painting of the white silk dress here—which is set off by the rusts and purples of the background clothing and by the woman's own short blue cloak.

Antoine Watteau *La Gamme d'Amour* · Oil on canvas · 20 ×
23½″ · National Gallery, London

In Watteau's pictures music is the food of love—and also its
language. Here the duet of the singer and her accompanist
becomes more than a musical harmony, as they exchange glances.
The pair of lovers is detached from the group in the background,
isolated in the moment of discovering their own emotions.
Watteau uses landscape in the same way that he does music, to
suggest the natural and the free. Out of doors there is no con-
straint, no formality. His clothes too are easier than the actual
clothes of the period—their fancy-dress version of seventeenth-
century costume represents one more emancipation from convention. His people naturally prefer to sit at their ease, in
flowing, graceful costumes, in sheltered parks and gardens. Yet,
with all this beauty, there goes some sense of the passage of time.
Love will not last forever. And here the antique stone bust seems
a reminder that stone can survive when human beings and their
passions have passed.

ANTOINE WATTEAU *The Concert* · c. 1716 · Oil on canvas · $25\frac{5}{8} \times 36\frac{5}{8}''$ · The Wallace Collection, London

Although he was never to visit Italy, Watteau was haunted by the great Italians—the Venetians, above all. He may well have known Giorgione's *Concert Champêtre* which was already in the French royal collection. That picture is the first large-scale statement of the twin theme of music and the countryside. It is, as it were, restated by Watteau's *Concert* where now a whole family are music-making or at least sharing in the musical atmosphere. The curled-up dog is certainly borrowed from Rubens—Watteau's other great source. But whereas it had been used by Rubens in his pageant of the *Coronation of Marie de' Medici*, Watteau places it in this relaxed, informal scene. This is how society now sees itself: placed as it were between interior and exterior, between art and nature. Watteau's are the most civilized pictures in a highly civilized century. 147

ANTOINE WATTEAU *Gilles* · 1719–21 · Oil on canvas · 72½ × 58¾″
· The Louvre, Paris

In this picture Watteau manages to suggest both the lively atmosphere of the comedians' performances and something of the life of
a comedian. The noisy fun of the background, where a clown is
pulled along on a donkey, is abruptly silenced by the complete
detachment and stillness of Gilles himself, at once dignified and
poignant. His expression is inscrutably blank. Yet he seems to
communicate to the spectator an intense and moving sense of
148 existence.

NICOLAS LANCRET (1690–1743) *Scene from the Italian Comedy* ·
Oil on canvas · 11 × 14⅛″ · The Wallace Collection, London

Nicolas Lancret pays tribute to the popularity of Watteau,
whose style of picture he was to continue. Lancret is a charming
painter, but most of Watteau's intensity and conviction has been
lost from his work and the content becomes rather anecdotal.
Scene from the Italian Comedy suffers from the fact that Watteau
had interpreted such scenes with pure enchantment. Lancret
remains a lively artist, with sensitive handling of the medium and
his own attractive color hamonies. The theater continued to
fascinate society during the period, and there was a natural
preference for amusing, amorous plays, as opposed to the
somewhat stilted, high-flown world of tragedy.   149

FRANÇOIS BOUCHER (1703–70) *Birth of Venus* · Oil on canvas · $31\frac{1}{2} \times 53\frac{7}{8}''$ · The Wallace Collection, London

François Boucher is more than the contemporary of Tiepolo. He is the Tiepolo of France, substituting fancy for imagination, but remaining a great decorative painter unjustly despised in the Neoclassic period in which he lived. His *Birth of Venus* tells us nothing about classical mythology. It is as a subject only the pretext for an attractive woman to recline in some not very realistic water. The light touch and delightful color enhance its pleasurable effect. What had originally been a rather brutal story of how Venus was born, became in Renaissance times an idyl of a goddess-woman floating over the water and eventually, with Boucher, the story is told in intimate, boudoir terms.

150

FRANÇOIS BOUCHER *The Bath of Diana* · Oil on canvas · 22½ ×
28¾″ · The Louvre, Paris

The patrons of Boucher, whether men or women, expected him
to pay tribute to the century's obsession with women. He is
virtually the inventor of a certain female type, with prettified
baby features and a body at once slim and mature. His mythological pictures revolve around this type of woman, shown either
titillatingly half-dressed or—as here—quite frankly nude. Boucher's response to blond flesh was very real, and here he sets
it off ravishingly with the great expanses of blue drapery and
green foliage. The picture is quite consciously artificial, but it is
also enchanting. Firmly planned and firmly executed, it is one of
Boucher's most serious masterpieces.

François Boucher *Nude on a Sofa* · 1752 · Oil on canvas · $23\frac{5}{8} \times 25\frac{3}{8}''$ · Alte Pinakothek, Munich

For a long while this picture was supposed to represent an Irish girl, Louise O'Murphy, who was one of the many mistresses of Louis XV. Her identity is of little importance, but Boucher has given her the ideal sensuousness, and sensuality, of an ideal mistress. Her pose and the disarray of clothes and sofa on which she lies might all have been thought up by Colette, so intense is the delight in the juxtaposed textures and so deep the sense of abandonment. Boucher is frank in his enjoyment of the subject. He means us to confound art and nature in this provocative portrait of a naked girl. She is not shown in any mythological guise but simply as herself. Boucher localized the picture in his own period and produced one of the finest nudes painted in the eighteenth century.

JEAN-HONORÉ FRAGONARD (1732–1806) *Rinaldo and Armida* ·
Oil on canvas · 28¾ × 35⅞″ · Private collection

Jean-Honoré Fragonard leads inevitably toward the dissolution
of the Rococo style. Pictures like *Rinaldo and Armida* fracture the
firm world of Boucher under new impact of light which sparkles
and breaks up all the surfaces—rather as Canaletto's world is
broken up by the light and rapid calligraphy of Guardi. With
nervous feathery strokes Fragonard creates a flickering composition in which everything seems excited. The figures are so many
curving strokes that reel and bound toward each other in a
frothy woodland setting. Rinaldo is led forward into the bowers
of the enchantress Armida. It is the same subject that Tiepolo had
already painted (page 129), and Tiepolo was one of the significant
influences on Fragonard.

JEAN-HONORÉ FRAGONARD *Bathers* · Before 1756 · Oil on canvas ·
25¼ × 32½″ · The Louvre, Paris

Although Fragonard pays tribute, like Boucher, to his period's
preoccupation with the feminine, it is with more dynamic effects.
Where Boucher, for example, had painted Diana almost pensively
at her bath (page 151), Fragonard conceives this animated and
erotic scene of bathers who tumble and fall about in the water.
Even the trees seem agitated by gusts of passion, and yet the
whole picture is lighthearted. Fragonard seems to go on painting
with tremendous verve and gaiety, keeping clear of too solemn
subject matter, and unaware that he would live on in penury and
154 neglect to see Napoleon on the throne of France.

JEAN-HONORÉ FRAGONARD *The Washerwoman* · c. 1756–67 · Oil on canvas · 18½ × 25⅝″ · Picardy Museum, Amiens

There is another aspect of Fragonard's art besides his cheerfully erotic vein. He won the Prix de Rome in 1752 and lived in Italy for some years. The romantic associations of Italy, its climate, its gardens, its statues, made a deep impression on him and he recorded them in wonderfully evocative drawings and paintings. *The Washerwoman* seems redolent of southern life with its sense of sunshine and dark trees, statues and a steep overgrown staircase. Everything is conveyed with sketchlike rapidity and the result is like a drawing in paint.

HUBERT ROBERT (1733–1808) *The Pont du Gard* · c. 1787 · Oil on canvas · 95 × 95″ · The Louvre, Paris

Hubert Robert influenced Fragonard (in such pictures as the one on page 155) and was in turn influenced by him. Robert, too, studied in Rome and became, in effect, a French version of the Roman view-painter, Panini. But there is in hem also a fully developed Romantic feeling which looks forward to the nineteenth century. The grandeur and the melancholy of ruins became his special subject. It was in front of one of his pictures that Diderot was to be led into musing on all the ideas that ruins evoked: *"Tout s'anéantit, tout périt, tout passe."* The double arches of the Pont du Gard seem to dwarf people into insignificance, stretched dramatically across the picture under a boldly 156 colored sky.

JEAN-BAPTISTE-SIMÉON CHARDIN (1699–1779) *The Morning Toilet* ·
Oil on canvas · 19¼ × 15⅜″ · National Museum, Stockholm

Jean-Baptiste-Siméon Chardin must have studied Dutch seventeenth-century pictures, but his own still lifes and genre scenes
have a dignity and power of composition that link them to
Poussin. Chardin manages to cut away all the trivial, anecdotal
qualities from his pictures and present us with much more than a
mere "slice of life." He prefers the interior on a small scale,
usually with only one or two figures who are occupied in some
simple domestic task. Here a mother gives the finishing touches
to her daughter's toilet before church. But the spell of the picture
is in its grave preoccupation and in the beautifully applied paint
which gives weight, as well as color, to each object. 157

JEAN-BAPTISTE-SIMÉON CHARDIN *The Kitchenmaid* · Oil on canvas · 18⅛ × 14¾″ · National Gallery of Art, Washington, D.C. (The Samuel H. Kress Collection)

Chardin, the contemporary of Boucher, takes us behind that gallant, Rococo façade and shows us the actual facts of existence of the period. Like the Rococo painters, he places the emphasis upon women—but with what a difference. Women are seen in the humblest circumstances, occupied in domestic tasks in the kitchen. Here a maid simply sits peeling turnips, or rather pauses for a moment in her work. This stillness is part of Chardin's quiet power. He checks the Rococo tendency to movement and dissolution, and makes all his pictures become literally still lifes. With immense gravity he examines each object, its essence and its surface, and records the vegetables, the pots and pans, the 158 shape of the woman's white apron.

JEAN-BAPTISTE-SIMÉON CHARDIN *Pipes and Drinking Vessels* ·
Oil on canvas · 12⅝ × 16½″ · The Louvre, Paris

Chardin began as a painter of still lifes and only gradually went
on to deal with genre compositions. In his later work he largely
left aside genre and turned back with new virtuosity to still life.
The actual elements remain simple and very much the same. The
composition is restricted to a few objects, usually placed—as
here—on a plain stone ledge that runs parallel with the bottom
of the picture. On this the objects are arranged with scrupulous
care; their varied shapes are plotted with exactness. The result is
the tremendous authority which exhales from Chardin's still lifes.
A few commonplace objects are lifted into a timeless plane. 159

JEAN-BAPTISTE-SIMÉON CHARDIN *Girl with a Racket and Shuttlecock*
· 1741 · Oil on canvas · 37⅞ × 24¼″ · Private collection, Paris

By the 1740s Chardin's art had become completely confident. Only then did he paint several pictures in which the human figure takes on, for him, a new and important scale. But the mood remains very much the same. He still concentrates on private domestic moments. Even when his subject is a child, it is the child's gravity which is portrayed. There is a touching solemnity about the girl who is absorbed in her own thoughts as she clasps the racket and shuttlecock. These shapes, like that made by her dress and by her profile against the cool background, are all explored and expressed with intense conviction. Only Vermeer has approached Chardin in that sense of light which saturates as it falls, building up surfaces of beauty like that of the girl's skirt.

Jean-Etienne Liotard (1702–89) *Self-Portrait* · Pastel · 24¾ × 20⅝" · Museum of Art and History, Geneva

Jean-Etienne Liotard was perhaps the most gifted in sheer virtuosity of all the eighteenth-century practitioners in the popular medium of pastel. He was Swiss by birth but traveled all over Europe, as well as to Turkey. His adoption of Turkish dress and growth of a beard added to his notoriety and in this portrait he well conveys a sense of his own eccentricity. The medium of pastel encouraged dexterity and speed—those qualities so much admired by the eighteenth century—and the pastel portrait was popular throughout Europe. Liotard aimed not so much at a lively touch as at *trompe l'œil* realism in conveying textures, combined with a powerful honesty in portraying his sitters—not least in this portrait of himself.

JEAN-MARC NATTIER (1685–1766) *Madame Henriette* · 1742 ·
Oil on canvas · $37\frac{1}{8} \times 50\frac{5}{8}''$ · Uffizi Gallery, Florence

Jean-Marc Nattier began his career as court portraitist with this
composition of Louis XV's daughter, painted in 1742. The eldest
of the king's children and much loved, she was to die at twenty-
four years of age in 1752. For this first of his portraits of her,
Nattier has lightly allegorized her into Flora or, rather, a nymph
who is weaving a crown of flowers. Portrayed like this, Madame
Henriette is able to adopt an unconventional but elegant pose,
very different from that of formal court portraiture. Nattier is
able to combine grace with a tolerable likeness. It is not surprising
that the portrait pleased the royal family, and the painter was to
go on to portray Madame Henriette's sisters as well as the king
162 and queen.

MAURICE QUENTIN DE LA TOUR (1704–88) *Self-Portrait* · 1751 ·
Pastel · 22 × 17⅝" · The Louvre, Paris

Maurice Quentin de La Tour was the leading French pastelist
of the period, approached only by Perronneau. Originally influenced by the success of the Venetian, Rosalba Carriera, La
Tour was to carry much further the vivacity of handling and
grasp of character. He was capable of great elaboration and
finish—in which pastel almost becomes paint—but it is in the
more relaxed and direct sketches and informal portraits that he
is at his best. Here he poses without any pretense—without wig
or formal cravat—simply as the artist-workman. He is able to
catch too the smiling, no-nonsense air of his own face, a good
guide to his character. An anecdote tells how, when painting
Madame de Pompadour, he undid his collar and took off his wig,
so as to feel completely at ease.

163

JEAN-BAPTISTE PERRONNEAU (1715–83) *Charles Lenormant du Coudray* · 1766 · Pastel · 24⅜ × 19″ · Cognacq-Jay Museum, Paris

Jean-Baptiste Perronneau cannot really equal La Tour in penetration as a portrait painter, but he was a successful artist of the period and worked in oils as well as pastel. Unlike La Tour, he was Parisian by birth but his later years took him wandering—perhaps to seek clients beyond La Tour's reach. He visited Italy and Russia and spent considerable periods in Amsterdam, where he died. The Lenormant portrait shows his ability as interpreter of character and physiognomy, and also contains a brilliant passage of that blue that Perronneau was so fond of introducing into his portraits.

JEAN-BAPTISTE GREUZE (1725–1805) *Head of a Child* · Oil on canvas · $16\frac{1}{4} \times 12\frac{5}{8}''$ · Kenwood Collection, London

Jean-Baptiste Greuze is an example of the artist whose historical importance is greater than his artistic merit. Launched by Diderot's high praise for his sentimental genre pictures, Greuze represents the triumph of bourgeois feeling and the rejection of the Rococo. But while it is still hard to appreciate the painter of the tearful village scenes which made him so famous (such as *The Village Bride*), and even less the creator of rouged girls posed with doves and jugs, it is necessary to recognize that Greuze was always an admirable portraitist. At his best and most straightforward, he was able to respond to children with real feeling, and their popularity in his work is part of the new urge toward a more natural code of manners. Greuze heralded the Revolution without being aware of doing so.

ELISABETH VIGÉE-LEBRUN (1755–1842) *Queen Marie-Antoinette* ·
Oil on canvas · $35\frac{3}{8} \times 28\frac{3}{8}''$ · Collection H.R.H. The Prince of
Hesse and the Rhine

Elisabeth Vigée-Lebrun became famous for her portraits of
Marie-Antoinette which represent a minor revolution in the
portrayal of royalty. Friendly with the Queen, Madame Vigée-
Lebrun was easily able to convey a simplicity and intimacy in her
portraits of a sovereign whose lack of formality shocked the
French court. In 1783 Marie-Antoinette adopted a new fashion
by wearing simple dresses of white muslin. It is in this costume
that she appears here, wearing a straw hat which adds a further
suggestion of the pastoral. In fact the portrait is a tacit recog-
nition that queens are really only ordinary women under the
trappings. The portrait had to be withdrawn from public ex-
166 hibition after its informality had caused a scandal.

PIERRE-PAUL PRUD'HON (1758–1823) *The Empress Josephine* · Oil
on canvas · 96 × 70½″ · The Louvre, Paris

Pierre-Paul Prud'hon, born only three years later than Madame
Vigée-Lebrun, carries further those hints of a new feeling which
her portraits contain. It is positively as an escape from rationality
and regal convention that Prud'hon's Josephine has seated herself in this romantic, lovely spot. She is an attractive if shadowy
figure—somebody whose charm still exerts itself over the years.
Prud'hon catches her easy elegance and natural grace, while the
woodland setting he places around her has the glowing beauty of
a landscape painted by Corot.

Jacques-Louis David (1748–1825) *The Oath of the Horatii* (detail)
· 1785 · Oil on canvas · 152 × 204¾″ · The Louvre, Paris

Jacques-Louis David painted *The Oath of the Horatii* in 1785, four
years before the French Revolution. The picture created a
sensation first in Rome—where it was painted—and then on its
exhibition in Paris. Its stern republican sentiment is foreboding,
both artistically and politically, and it is a pleasing irony that the
commission for it came from the Crown. The subject was inspired
by Corneille's tragedy, *Horace*. Although there is some lingering
theatricality in David's treatment, he has aimed at a dramatic
moment interpreted by a static composition. It is a solemn
moment of action frozen in the uplifted arms, the static folds of
the draperies, and the regular series of arches that enclose the
background. All the nascent and confused ideas of Neoclassicism
168 are suddenly given complete, coherent expression.

JAQUES-LOUIS DAVID *Madame Récamier* · Oil on canvas · 67 ×
94½″ · The Louvre, Paris

Significantly, it was in 1800 that David began this famous portrait
of a famous beauty, which he never completed. The picture is
exactly balanced between two centuries. Despite the classic
severity of the composition, it places an almost Rococo feminine
emphasis upon woman herself: Madame Récamier seems to
incarnate womanhood, so beautiful, so tantalizing, so consciously
exerting her charm. In the masculine, politically realistic world
of Napoleon, she still remains a goddess and an enchantress. No
longer posed as Cleopatra or Armida, she is simply one ordinary
woman, Jeanne-Françoise Récamier. And it is in this sense of
being "modern" that David is a revolutionary. The bareness
of the room, the austerity of the clothes and furniture, all symbol-
ize rejection of the Rococo.

JACQUES-LOUIS DAVID *Napoleon in His Study* · Oil on canvas
$80\frac{1}{4} \times 49\frac{1}{4}''$ · National Gallery of Art, Washington, D.C.

The Napoleonic legend, created so assiduously by Napoleon,
needed pictorial expression, and it was fortunate for the Emperor
that a perfect court artist-cum-propagandist was available in
David. Not only did David respond with complete loyalty to
Napoleon, but he has enshrined the man and his ideals in a whole
series of portraits. Here, the Emperor stands in his study in his
habitual pose. It is a deliberately private scene, an intimate view
of the man who early in the morning—the clock shows it is
nearly a quarter past four—is still at work. The candles have
burned low, but France's destiny requires the constant toil of her
master.

WILLIAM HOGARTH (1697–1764) *The Shrimp Girl* · c. 1750–60 ·
Oil on canvas · 26 × 20¾″ · National Gallery, London

William Hogarth began by painting small portraits and conver-
sation pieces, but was led from these to the idea of depicting
"modern moral subjects" in a way that anticipates Greuze.
Hogarth's deep attachment to the ordinary life of the period is
summed up in this "portrait" of an itinerant shrimp girl—a
cockney character rather like the painter himself. The picture is
only a sketch and is perhaps unfinished. Nevertheless, it is
completely realized and painted with almost Impressionist
freedom.

WILLIAM HOGARTH *The Graham Children* · 1742 · Oil on canvas · $63\frac{3}{4} \times 71\frac{1}{4}''$ · The Tate Gallery, London

Hogarth's lively attitude made him a naturally sympathetic portraitist of children. In *The Graham Children* he paints them in a group portrait on a large scale. He aims at the informality of a moment of their daily life, here focused on the pet bird in the cage which has caught the attention of the baby at the left. Round the children is depicted a complete interior of the period, where the only contrived element is a swag of curtain. Amid the bright-eyed, eager-looking children there is also set the bright-eyed cat which—equally attracted by the bird—has popped up from behind the chair. It is perhaps the liveliest sitter of all.

RICHARD WILSON (1713/14–82) *View of Snowdon* · Oil on canvas ·
$39\frac{5}{8} \times 48\frac{7}{8}''$ · The Walker Art Gallery, Liverpool

Richard Wilson was to move from portrait painting to the depiction of landscapes, influenced by several seventeenth-century
masters and also by his contemporary Zuccarelli. Wilson's visit
to Italy in the 1750s resulted in this switch of subject matter and
his Italian views have a strong sense of classical nostalgia—as
well as a classical gravity in their design. The same Italian and
classicizing vein was to be utilized by him in approaching scenes
in England and in his native Wales. A glowing light gives
dignity to the landscape where some simple feature of grandeur
—as here the peak of Snowdon—takes its place boldly in the
composition. Wilson's elevated view of nature found fewer
patrons at the time than the sugary and more flimsy landscapes
painted by Zuccarelli.

GEORGE STUBBS (1724–1806) *Mares and Foals* · c. 1760–70 · Oil on canvas · 40 × 63¼″ · The Tate Gallery, London

George Stubbs is one of those artists of the eighteenth century who reveal how deeply imbued the period was with scientific interests. In Stubbs art serves knowledge, and for him it is knowledge especially of the animal kingdom—and particularly, knowledge of the horse. He dissected horses and drew the results of his study, in addition to painting many horse portraits. Behind all of them is a sense of bone and structure which helps to give tremendous conviction to the individual studies here; at the same time, together they make up a delightful decorative frieze, which is charming as well as natural, true to the facts and yet essentially poetic.

SIR JOSHUA REYNOLDS (1723–92) *The Strawberry Girl* · Oil on canvas · 29¼ × 24¾″ · The Wallace Collection, London

Sir Joshua Reynolds is the leading figure, historically, in the eighteenth-century English School. He painted nothing but portraits and nearly every leading figure of the period sat to him. He represents a tremendous advance in the social prestige of the painter, accelerated by the creation of the Royal Academy in 1768. Reynolds, its first President, was knighted by George III. As well as attempting every variety of treatment of his sitters, Reynolds was attracted to the "fancy picture" with a possible classical or genre interest. *The Strawberry Girl* is at once portrait and genre, painted with clear recollections of Murillo, and patently sentimental when compared with Hogarth's depiction of children.

SIR JOSHUA REYNOLDS *Nelly O'Brien* · c. 1760–62 · Oil on canvas ·
49¾ × 39¼″ · The Wallace Collection, London

Although Reynolds was quite capable of classicizing his sitters
—especially female ones—and providing them with classical
draperies, he could also create startlingly direct and "modern"
portraits. *Nelly O'Brien* is a supreme example of this more sympathetic vein; her portrait may be contrasted with the elaborate full-
length of Lady Bampfylde (page 178). Reynolds was a friend of
Nelly O'Brien's, who was a courtesan of the period. The portrait
breathes affection and simplicity. The pose is deliberately direct
and straightforward, in a manner very unusual for Reynolds.
Equally unusual is his sensitive recording of the varied textures
of her clothes, from the lace at her sleeves to the striped dress
—partly covered by a black shawl—and the beautifully painted
176 quilted skirt which fills the foreground.

SIR JOSHUA REYNOLDS *Lord Heathfield* · 1787 · Oil on canvas · 56 × 44¾″ · National Gallery, London

There is something retiring in Reynolds' concept of Nelly O'Brien. Lord Heathfield was a public and important person, and this aspect of him is seized on in Reynolds' impressive portrait. Lord Heathfield was the governor of Gibraltar and had sustained a famous siege of the island. He holds the key of the fortress, while in the background there smokes the cannon which defended Gibraltar. Bluff, confident, a hero but not posing in any conventionally heroic way, Lord Heathfield is presented as no more than a man—but also as a personality. It is with this kind of dominating male sitter that Reynolds was probably most successful.

Sir Joshua Reynolds *Lady Bampfylde* · 1776/77 · Oil on canvas
93¾ × 58¼″ · The Tate Gallery, London

Reynolds was capable of changing to suit the type of sitter and
the purpose of the portrait. *Lady Bampfylde* is the aristocrati
extreme: a full-length of contrived grace, attired in those mock
simple clothes that were sometimes stigmatized by Reynolds
contemporaries as "nightgowns." Everything about her is per
haps rather too fluid and beautiful to be true—from the sinuou
line of her white scarf to the profusion of lilies so surprisingl
growing in a wood. The sitter herself seems not positive enoug
to carry off all these trappings, despite all Reynolds' contrivance

THOMAS GAINSBOROUGH (1727–88) *The Painter's Daughters Chasing a Butterfly* · c. 1755/56 · Oil on canvas · $44\frac{1}{2} \times 41\frac{3}{8}''$ · National Gallery, London

Thomas Gainsborough is in eternal contrast to Reynolds. Comtemporaries, portraitists, acquaintances, and at the end virtually friends, they had very different aims and ambitions. It can be said that Reynolds is all talent, Gainsborough genius. While Reynolds continually strives, Gainsborough achieves his effects with easy mastery. He is the creator of a whole series of felicitous masterpieces, but even among them few reach the lyrical level of is portrait of his two daughters, Mary and Margaret. The picture shows a completely absorbed moment of childhood, as the children run through the trees, intent on the butterfly. The paint uns too, rapidly conveying the shadowy wood, the silver-lemon one of the girls' dresses, and their solemn, dark-eyed faces. 179

THOMAS GAINSBOROUGH *Mary, Countess Howe* · Oil on canvas · 96 × 60″ · The London County Council, Iveagh Bequest, Kenwood

Gainsborough was a countryman by birth, and he kept a sort of rustic disrespect before even his grandest sitters. Lady Howe, the wife of a distinguished sailor also painted by Gainsborough, is dressed for the country, with gloves and a wide-brimmed straw hat. Over her marvelously painted raspberry-pink dress, she wears a nearly transparent muslin apron, very slightly agitated. The same slight current seems to shake the slender trees of the delicate landscape where she stands. All these details are part of Gainsborough's spontaneous delight in costume and in 180 motion.

THOMAS GAINSBOROUGH *The Morning Walk* · 1785 · Oil on canvas · 93 × 70″ · National Gallery, London

This portrait is among Gainsborough's last pictures and shows a young, newly married couple, Mr. and Mrs. William Hallett. They stroll in a wood which Gainsborough has turned into an enchanted bower of silk and feathers—rather like the plumes and ribbon of Mrs. Hallett's hat. There is a graceful sense of movement as the couple walk along, arms interlinked, and accompanied by their elegant, silky-furred dog. By this date Gainsborough's handling of oil paint had become even more fluent. He worked with long brushes and achieved effects almost like penciling.

THOMAS GAINSBOROUGH *The Ford* · Before 1786 · Oil on canvas
$38\frac{7}{8} \times 49''$ · Collection Mrs. H. Scudamore, London

Gainsborough differed in yet another way from Reynolds in
being a painter of landscapes as well as portraits. Already as a
boy he was painting, under Dutch influence, scenes of his native
Suffolk. Later in life he preferred to paint half-imaginary landscapes, concocted from pieces of twig and stones which he would
arrange in his studio. A haze of enchantment gradually comes
over his landscapes, just as it does over his portraits. The sober
depiction of actual reality is replaced by a lighter and more
graceful interpretation in which the trees group themselves
elegantly and the peasants take on almost the grace of dancers. In
these landscapes it is easy to see affinities with Fragonard—whose
182 work Gainsborough probably did not know.

WILLIAM BLAKE (1757–1827) *The Simoniac Pope* · c. 1825 · Pen
and watercolor · 20⅝ × 14¼″ · The Tate Gallery, London

William Blake seems to fit into the eighteenth century no more
easily than does David or Goya. Certainly he was violently
antagonistic to all the Rococo and divine-right-of-kings para-
phernalia. He asserts the artist's right to his own private visions,
reinforced in his own case by great poetic gifts—arguably
greater than his gifts as an artist. Most of his work was executed
in watercolor or engraving, and with an increasing attachment
to the purely visionary. His subjects were taken either from his
own poems, or from the Book of Job, or—as here—from Dante. 183

SIR THOMAS LAWRENCE (1769–1830) *Queen Charlotte* · Oil on canvas · 94¼ × 58″ · National Gallery, London

Sir Thomas Lawrence was brilliantly precocious, and he was still a young man when he painted this portrait of Queen Charlotte. It reveals his bravura qualities and also his ability to invest his sitters with glamour as well as dignity. The homely queen is not flattered as she sits high up in a room at Windsor Castle looking out over Eton—the chapel of which is visible among the russet autumn trees. Yet there is a stateliness in the presentation which suits the sitter. Out of her basically simple dress, Lawrence makes a beautiful piece of crisp painting, a sweep of pale lilac which heightens the effect of distance and dignity.

184

Sir Henry Raeburn (1756–1823) *The Drummond Children* · Oil on canvas · 94¼ × 60¼″ · Metropolitan Museum of Art, New York

Sir Henry Raeburn was to become the leading portrait painter in Edinburgh, influenced by Reynolds and living on into the age of Lawrence. He seems to have received little early training, but developed a virtuoso handling of oil paint which often becomes rather monotonous in its slick application. Already there is a hint of Victorian sentimentality in his portraits of children, although *The Drummond Children* is more elaborately worked out than usual and an extremely effective group.

Luis Meléndez (1716–80) *Still Life with Pears and a Melon*
Oil on canvas · $15\frac{7}{8} \times 20\frac{1}{2}''$ · Museum of Fine Arts, Boston

Luis Meléndez was probably ambitious to be known as a history
painter and in his own self-portrait he shows himself holding an
academic drawing. However, he is famous for his still-life
pictures which in many ways continue the tradition of Velázquez
and Zurbarán. At the same time, it is interesting to find him
insisting on the sheer facts of objects—concentrating deeply on
their appearance—in the very years that Chardin was at work in
Paris. There is a conscious austerity about Meléndez' pictures.
Here each pear seems scrutinized and recorded with minute
accuracy, and in the same way the tough texture of the melon
skin is explored. The fruit is placed in full light and set off by the
very simple vessels and the basket, with its sharp white drapery,
186 which have an almost inexplicable, innate dignity.

Francisco Goya (1746–1828) *The Duchess of Alba* · 1795 · Oil
on canvas · 74¾ × 51⅛″ · Collection Duke of Alba, Madrid

Francisco Goya not only revives the great tradition of Spanish
painting but positively leads painting into the nineteenth century.
That his death was in France is almost symbolic, as if in rec-
ognition of the country that was to continue in the creation of
modern art. From Goya it is a logical step to Géricault and
Delacroix. This portrait was painted in 1795 and is only one
testimony to the artist's fascination with a woman who was
described as "outstanding for her beauty, popularity, charm,
riches, and rank."

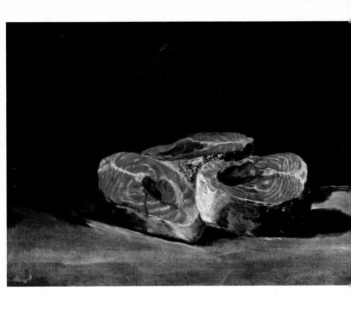

FRANCISCO GOYA *Still Life with Salmon* · Oil on canvas · 17⅝ ×
24⅜″ · Collection Dr. Oskar Reinhart, Winterthur

It is a part of Goya's modernity that he tackled all subjects.
Though his still-life pictures are few they provide further
testimony to his delight in the topical subject. He was least
successful in the world of myth and allegory, and superb when
it came to grasping in paint or ink the world of actuality. Out of
a few collops of salmon he is able to make this impressive picture
which conveys the raw red flesh of the fish and the mottled shiny
grayish skin which so vividly contrasts with it. There is hardly
any arrangement of the three pieces: they are simply laid in the
center of the composition and then painted with tremendous
respect for the sheer facts. The boldness of the concept and the
execution once again prelude the entire nineteenth century and,
188 here especially, Courbet.

FRANCISCO GOYA *Majas on a Balcony* · c. 1810–15 · Oil on canvas ·
76¾ × 49½″ · Metropolitan Museum of Art, New York

The life of his own time fascinated Goya and the present picture
shows an almost idyllic and charming scene of social life in the
Madrid of about 1800. There is really no subject. It is merely an
impression of contemporary life—as if the artist had glanced up
in a Madrid street and seen these four people sitting out on a
balcony. The actual painting is direct and vivid, with masterly
touches just suggesting the women's veils. Not only does its
technique prelude Manet, but even its subject is likely to have
inspired his famous picture *Le Balcon*.

Francisco Goya *Self-Portrait* · 1785 · Oil on canvas · 16½ ×
10″ · Collection of the Count of Vallagonzalo, Madrid

Goya's interest in life around him naturally included himself.
Indeed, his highly conscious art depends on a great deal of self-
awareness and probably no artist has probed as deeply as did he
into the mind and its mental states. He was still comparatively
young when this full-scale self-portrait was painted—a completely
revolutionary conception in its silhouetting of the figure against
the light expanse of the window. It shows Goya as he supremely
thought of himself: as an active artist.

FRANCISCO GOYA *The Third of May, 1808* · c. 1814 · Oil on canvas · 104¾ × 135⅞″ · The Prado, Madrid

The confused events which followed on France's invasion of Spain are made almost intolerably vivid by two pictures which Goya painted some five years after the actual events. On May 2, the Spanish rose against Napoleon's troops and attacked them in the streets of Madrid. Goya painted that scene. The following day French reprisals resulted in the scene depicted here when hostages were shot. In a dark night, these pitiful figures cluster together before the level, lethal line of French rifles. One man screams in defiance, and despair perhaps, as the soldiers shoot. Already blood stains the ground where the first victims have fallen. Goya's attachment to reality continued even before such spectacles as this. He does not seem to indict the French so much as he does man's brutality to man. The eighteenth century, which had thought to laugh man's follies away, was condemned to see its civilized system collapse. Goya shows its death agony.

191

FRANCISCO GOYA *The Colossus (Panic)* · 1809 · Oil on canvas ·
76¾ × 41⅜″ · The Prado, Madrid

In his later years Goya did not retreat from reality but he turned
from man's exterior behavior to study more intensely man's mind.
Always interested in, and aware of, the basic irrationality which
is waiting to engulf the structure of reason, Goya was increasingly
preoccupied by dreams and by visions of nightmarish intensity.
Many of the resulting "black paintings" he intended for the
decoration of his own house—extensions as it were of what his
mind had already dreamed. The subjects of these pictures are
horrific and mysterious. Sanity seems to have deserted the earth
and it is inhabited by giant forms like this one which has terrified
a great crowd of people. Men are reduced to panicky little
creatures—ants frightened by the colossal figure which rises so
huge into the clouds. Thus the last eighteenth-century artist ends
not with charming pictures, or graceful decorations, but with
this dreadful vision of the world gone mad.

ACKNOWLEDGMENTS

The following photographers, phographic agencies, and pub-
ishers have co-operated in the making and gathering of the color
photographs for this book:

La Photothèque, Paris; Photographie Giraudon, Paris;
Scala Istituto Fotografico Editoriale, Florence.

The publisher and the author express their gratitude and appreciation to all the museums, galleries, cultural authorities, and
private collectors who so graciously made available for this book
the works in their custody or possession. All such sources are
acknowledged in the captions for the individual reproductions.

17th & 18th CENTURY PAINTING

El Greco, Rembrandt, Rubens, Velázquez, Gainsborough, Goya — these are only a few of the great seventeenth- and eighteenth-century masters whose paintings, celebrating and illuminating their times, bring those times vividly alive for us today. In this book are collected nearly 200 full-color illustrations of their works, and works by other artists of comparable genius. The accompanying text describes the basic elements of the major art styles of the period—the Baroque, Caravaggesque realism, Rococo, and Neoclassic.

COVER ILLUSTRATIONS:

LEFT: *Interior with Woman Holding a Glass*, *Pieter de Hooch*.

RIGHT: *The Bath of Diana*, *François Boucher*.

1968